Jed Smith

TRAILBLAZER OF THE WEST

by Frank Latham

—Revised and Edited by Michael J. McHugh—

A publication of
Christian Liberty Press
502 West Euclid Avenue
Arlington Heights, Illinois 60004

Revised and edited by Michael J. McHugh
Cover design by Bob Fine
Layout and graphics by Bob Fine
Illustrated by Frank Murch

Ad maiorem

Dei gloriam

CHRISTIAN LIBERTY PRESS
502 West Euclid Avenue
Arlington Heights, Illinois 60004
www.christianlibertypress.com

ISBN 1-930367-86-4

Printed in the United States of America

Contents

—Preface—

When students of American history study about the opening and settlement of the vast western wilderness territory, they often think of names such as Kit Carson, Lewis and Clark, and Zebulon Pike. Seldom will students be given the opportunity to learn about other individuals who contributed greatly to the process of westward expansion.

The book that follows tells the story of one man who deserves to be recognized for his outstanding contributions to the opening of the West in the nineteenth century—Jedediah Smith. The trailblazer known as Jed Smith (1799–1831) was a daring explorer, a skilled trapper, and a dedicated Christian frontiersman. As a young man, he dared to live his God-given dreams, and, as a result blazed a trail of achievement and honor throughout much of the West. His work literally opened up major portions of the wilderness territory to settlers traveling west of the Rocky Mountains.

Few men in American history experienced more intense challenges and outright danger than Jed Smith, the "knight in buckskin," and lived to tell about it. He was a truly courageous adventurer. Best of all, his story and Christian testimony are as amazing as they are true.

May the book that follows inspire readers to live out their own dreams, and ultimately, to adopt the Christian faith as their own.

Michael J. McHugh
2003

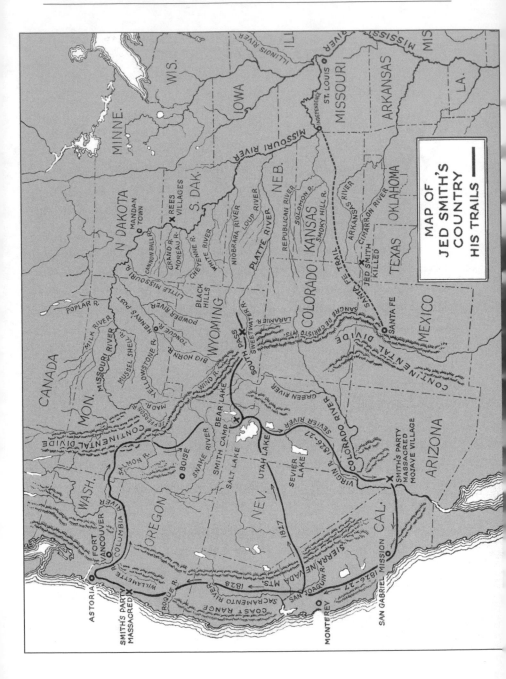

CHAPTER 1
Jed Wins a Fight

"Here, sonny, take a drink o' this. It'll tighten your scalp so Indians can't take it so easy when we go up the Missouri with Ashley."

Hank Johnson, mountain man, slapped a huge fist on the table as he spoke. Then he held a cup in front of young Jed Smith.

"No thank you. I don't drink," Jed said, shaking his head. "I promised my mother…"

"He promised his maw! Did you hear that, men?"

Johnson gave a short laugh as he looked around the room at the dozen mountain men sitting at tables. Like himself, all were dressed in buckskins. Like himself, all had heavy beards and long, tangled hair. Jed, with his face smooth-shaven and his brown hair neatly cut, looked very young among them.

Hank Johnson winked at the others. He thought he saw a chance for fun. "What are you doin' so far from your maw?" he asked, turning back to Jed. "Why in thunder did Ashley hire a youngin' who's still wet behind the ears?"

"Maybe Ashley wants you to nurse him," red-bearded Joe Holt spoke up.

"You know what I think," Johnson said. "I think a feller who won't take a drink is too yellow to go up the Missouri with us. He'd turn an' run the first time he heard a wolf howl." Again Hank held the cup out to Jed.

Jed could feel his heart pounding. He tried to smile, as he repeated, "No thank you. I don't care to drink. But I won't try to

force you to not drink. So that should make us even. There is no reason why we should quarrel about it."

"He don't care if I drink! Now, ain't that nice. I think," said Johnson, "I'd better take this yellow-belly in my arms and feed him outa my cup." With this, Johnson reached across the table and put a hairy hand on Jed's shoulder. "What you got to say to that?" he asked.

"Nothing," said Jed quietly, "except you better take your hand off my shoulder."

"I'm keeping my hand right where it is, yellow-belly," said Johnson. "Now what you got to say?"

"Nothing else," said Jed. Suddenly, he straightened up to his full six feet in height. His fist moved up from his side and hit Hank Johnson's jaw with a sound like an axe hitting a spruce log. Johnson's head snapped back and his feet went up in the air. The table turned violently on its side. Johnson fell full length on the floor and lay still.

"That'll be enough outa you!" yelled red-headed Joe Holt, leaping to his feet. Rushing at Jed, he tried to wrap his heavy arms around the lad, but Jed stepped back quickly. Holt missed a punch at Jed and stumbled. Then Jed's fist lashed out. It caught Holt between the eyes. The mountain man wobbled from side to side and fell flat on his face.

In an instant, Jed was surrounded by eight or ten mountain men. But now another man dressed in a dark business suit and tall hat was pushing through the crowd. "What is going on here?" he demanded.

A mountain man with a yellow beard and smiling eyes stepped forward. "Hello, General Ashley," he said pleasantly. "This lad just knocked out Johnson and Holt. It seems like Jed Smith didn't want to take a drink. But they wouldn't let him alone; so he cooled them off."

"All right, Black. Take a look at Johnson and Holt and see what the damage is," the general ordered. Then he turned to look at Jed, who was shifting his feet nervously, looking down at his skinned hand.

"Johnson's got a busted jaw," Art Black reported. "Holt has a busted nose. Otherwise, the boys are in fine shape."

"Two men laid up for repairs," said Ashley. "Is that a usual day's work for you, young man? Or do we have to expect more? It's still early in the evening."

"I'm sorry about this, General Ashley," Jed said. "I shouldn't have lost my temper. But I don't like to have any man say I'm a coward because I won't take a drink."

General Ashley didn't speak. He just stood looking at his new man, till finally Jed asked rather sharply, "Is drinking required on this trip, General Ashley?"

Ashley smiled. "If you can do your work on this trip, I don't care what you drink, Jed," he said. "You can even drink water. But take it easy if some of the boys make remarks. We'll be too busy trapping beaver and looking out for Indians to fix up men with broken jaws and noses."

Jed shifted uneasily from one foot to another, then suddenly said good night to General Ashley and followed Art out of the room.

For several minutes the two walked in silence along the rough street. Many times they bumped into men in the darkness. At last Art spoke.

"This town is getting too crowded with people to be comfortable." As Jed said nothing, Art continued to talk, trying to get his young companion to relax. "The newcomers are mostly trappers," he said. "French boatmen and merchants are big in the fur trade. Right now, St. Louis is the leading fur-trading town in the whole West. It's going to be an important city some day."

Jed still refused to talk, so Art finally touched his shoulder and asked, "What's eating at you, Jed? Don't keep on worrying about that fight. It's over and done with. You'll have no more trouble. When this news gets around, the boys are going to let you alone."

"I can't help having regrets about the fight," Jed answered. "It's the first time I ever really hurt a man with my fists, and I don't like it. What's more, I don't think the Almighty does either."

"Jed, a man sometimes has to let other men know that they can't push him too hard. It wasn't your fault that Hank and Joe tried to get rough with you."

"But I'm ashamed of myself," Jed said. "God didn't put men on the earth to snap at one another like wild dogs. There is much good work to be done on this earth before we leave it. And we can't do this work if we fight each other over minor offenses and name calling."

"Well," said Art, "all I've got to say is a young fellow with all these ideas in his head is likely to be mighty sad and lonesome. You're going to be in a wild country and live among rough men for the next two or three years. Are you sure that's what you want to do? You really want to go up the Missouri with us?"

"Yes, I do. I want to go," replied Jed firmly. "And I won't be lonesome when I get out there." He waved his hand toward the northwest. "There are a lot of white spaces on the maps of that unknown country. Someday, the United States is going to own the country beyond the Rocky Mountains. I want to see what's really out there—I've dreamed of seeing that country for so long."

CHAPTER 2

Jed Hears of Faraway Lands

Young Jedediah Strong Smith was born in Bainbridge, New York, January 6, 1799. His parents, Jedediah Smith and Sarah Strong Smith, were running a little store at Bainbridge the year Jed was born. But they did not stay long in New York State. Jed's father had the urge to keep moving farther west. First he moved to Pennsylvania, and then to Ohio.

By this time, there were eleven children in the Smith home. Sarah Strong Smith urged her husband to try to settle down in one place. She wanted her children to get the opportunity to attend a solid Christian church and to grow up in the company of God-fearing people.

There was no school near the Smiths in Ohio, but they found their children could get schooling just the same. Dr. Simons, who lived near them, didn't just take care of the sick. He also taught many of the children round about. Dr. Simons became especially fond of young Jed Smith, whom he tutored for quite some time.

The doctor would come home at night worn out from a long trip to visit a patient, and there would be Jed waiting eagerly for him. Jed's wanting to learn arithmetic, English, biblical theology, and history made Dr. Simons forget how tired he was.

One evening, Jed seemed to be particularly excited when he met Dr. Simons.

"This book you gave me, Dr. Simons, about the Lewis and Clark expedition. I want to talk more about it, please," Jed said. "How did we get that big country west of the Mississippi, the Louisiana Territory they went through? I'm ashamed to admit it, but I don't know much about the history of our country."

"Don't be ashamed because you don't know something, Jed. You need be ashamed only if you ever stop trying to learn more," said Dr. Simons.

"All right, let's talk about the Louisiana Territory. It stretches west from the Mississippi River to the Rocky Mountains. It runs from the Gulf of Mexico on the south to Canada on the north, and takes in the important port of New Orleans at the mouth of the Mississippi.

"Spain had held the Louisiana Territory for a long time," continued Dr. Simons. "But in 1800, Napoleon of France forced Spain to give Louisiana to France.

"This news worried Americans who lived along the Mississippi and Ohio rivers. They sold their farm crops in New Orleans, and they were afraid that France would not let Americans do business freely in that city. People who lived in Tennessee, Kentucky, and Ohio wanted to go to war and take New Orleans from France."

Dr. Simons paused while Jed took notes.

"Then," added Dr. Simons, "President Thomas Jefferson got busy. He did not want any war. But he did want to get control of New Orleans. So he sent his friend James Monroe to France to see if he could buy New Orleans from Napoleon. Monroe talked things over with Robert Livingston, the American minister to France. Monroe and the minister then went to see Napoleon, who really surprised them. Napoleon swept his hand over the map and offered to sell the whole Louisiana Territory to the United States."

"But why, why did he do that?" exclaimed Jed. "How could Napoleon do that? Didn't the people of France have anything to say about this?"

Dr. Simons laughed. "One question at a time, Jed. First, we must remember that what Napoleon said was law in France. The people could do nothing about it."

"But, why did Napoleon suddenly decide to sell the whole Louisiana Territory after he had just gotten it from Spain?" asked Jed.

"Napoleon was getting ready to fight England again," replied Dr. Simons. "He knew that England's navy could keep France from sending soldiers to New Orleans. This meant that France would lose the territory to England. So why not make some money by selling Louisiana before he lost it?" Dr. Simons added.

"Well, anyway, Napoleon sold the Louisiana Territory to us for around $15,000,000. The purchase of this land pushed our frontier 1,500 miles farther west. It made the Mississippi an American river and a safe water highway for our farmers and merchants.

"I say that the Louisiana Purchase was the greatest land bargain in the world. People back East think this territory is mostly rocks and forests. They say it is fit only for wild animals and a few hunters. But I believe it will one day be a rich land of farms and cities."

Jed was to learn that Dr. Simons was right about the value of the Louisiana Territory. The Louisiana Purchase more than doubled the area of the United States. It probably did more than anything else to make the United States a great and important nation.

The Louisiana Territory contained the areas, which were to become the states of Louisiana, Arkansas, Oklahoma, Missouri, Kansas, Nebraska, Iowa, North Dakota, South Dakota, and Montana. In time, Minnesota and parts of Colorado and Wyoming would also be made from this land.

Jed's eyes shone as he listened to the doctor. A longing awoke in him. It was as if that wonderful frontier beyond the Mississippi was calling to him. What really lay beyond the river, beyond the mountains? Some day he must find out for himself.

"Well, what is it, Jed?" Dr. Simons asked. "You act like you are full of questions again."

"Yes," said Jed. "There's so much I want to know. Tell me more about Lewis and Clark."

"First," said Dr. Simons, "you tell me what you know about them. Let me see how well you remember what you read."

"Well," said Jed, "President Jefferson was anxious to open the Louisiana Territory to settlers, so he ordered Meriwether Lewis and William Clark to explore it. He asked them to map a route up the Missouri River and across the Rocky Mountains and to describe the country they saw. Lewis and Clark started in the spring of 1804 and came back in the fall of 1806. They crossed the Rocky Mountains and then followed the Columbia River down to the Pacific Ocean."

"Correct," said Dr. Simons.

"But what about the country south of the Columbia River?" asked Jed. "Is there another way to cross the Rocky Mountains farther south?" Jed began to pace the room excitedly. "I have been looking at maps of that country. There are a lot of white spaces on them. I want to know what is in those white spaces. I want to go out there some day and find out!"

"Calm down, Jed," Dr. Simons laughed. "I'm sure you will find out what you want to know. Of course, you will have to wait until you are older. But you can prepare for your future calling by studying hard right now. Who knows, perhaps, in the providence of God, your life's work will be to explore unknown lands for the good of Christ and His Kingdom."

Dr. Simons paused, then in quite a new tone of voice he said, "We will take up our study of the Bible. Remember, Jed, no man will go far without the help of God and His Word. The Scriptures, my dear boy, will be as a lamp unto your feet and a light unto your path, if you will but apply God's wisdom to your heart."

Jed kept busy with his studies, but he was required to help his father clothe and feed a large family. He knew arithmetic and English, and that helped him to get a job as clerk on a Lake Erie freight boat. He was only fifteen, but he did a man's work.

Working on the freight boat, Jed heard the British fur traders talk about the fur business. They said a man could make a lot of money trapping beaver, if he did not get killed by Indians. The beaver's silky fur was needed to make men's tall hats. There was a big demand for it back East.

Jed also heard the traders and trappers talk about faraway rivers. They spoke of the Snake, the Yellowstone, the Musselshell, the Madison, the Jefferson, and the Gallatin rivers, where the mighty Missouri River begins. The names kept running through Jed's mind when he tried to go to sleep at night. Would he ever get to see those rivers?

For the next seven years, Jed continued working on Lake Erie freight boats. He spent much of his free time reading every book he could find about the Far West. He also visited Dr. Simons and had long talks with him about everything from theology to buffalo hunting.

The older Jed got, the more convinced he became that it was God's will for him to explore the white spaces on the maps of the Far West. But the folks at home still needed him, and Jed was determined to honor his mother and father. There were five younger brothers who had to be given a start in life, and Jed prayed for the grace to wait patiently for the opportunity to begin his life's work.

A year later, the time at last came for this young man to say farewell to this home and family. Jed made up his mind to leave for the West. He had heard the trappers say money was to be made in the fur trade if a man only had but little brains and a lot of courage. Jed hoped that he could make enough money in a year or two to help out his youngest brothers and his parents.

But Jed did not like to think too much about making money. Dr. Simons had said a lot of things about people who thought too much about money. "God seldom blesses such people," said the wise doctor. So Jed liked to think about the good he could accomplish by exploring the uncivilized areas of the West.

Those faraway lands were waiting for someone with courage enough to explore them, Jed thought. Maybe he would be the first man to see the southern country beyond the Rocky Mountains. Even the brave Lewis and Clark had never seen it. Jed talked with Dr. Simons about going, and the doctor said, "If it is God's will, you will be the man who explores that land."

On the day Jed left for the West, his father put both hands on his shoulders, and cleared his throat but couldn't say anything for some time. Finally, he told his son to lean upon the Lord for daily strength.

Sarah Strong Smith kissed her son and said, "I am not going

to send you away with tears in my eyes, Jed. And I am not going to give you a lot of advice on what to do. You have always been a boy that could be trusted to do the right thing. Keep your faith in God, Jed, and think of us back home."

Jed's eyes were misty as he said good-bye to his parents and walked down the road to Dr. Simons's house.

Upon arriving, the good doctor put a book of hymns in Jed's hand. "These songs will be a comfort to you in the wilderness," said Dr. Simons. "You are going to live in a wild land, Jed. You will meet many men who know little of God and are full of destructive habits. Don't give up your faith. Don't put your trust in men. Remember, you will go far if you always live by the grace of God."

"I understand, Dr. Simons. You will never be ashamed of what I do out there."

Jed put the book away in his pack and strapped the pack on his shoulders. He then picked up his rifle, shook hands with his old friend, and started on his way west.

It was the spring of 1822 when twenty-three year old Jed Smith arrived in St. Louis, a town of 5,000 on the edge of the wilderness. Jed was dressed in homespun clothes and carried a bag containing all he owned. His greatest treasures were his books: a Bible, the Methodist hymnbook, a history book, and his old book about the Lewis and Clark expedition.

Jed looked eagerly around him as he walked down the dusty streets. St. Louis seemed a great and wonderful city to him. It was exciting and filled with color. The streets by the water were crowded with bearded trappers dressed in buckskins, and with French boatmen wearing red woolen caps and shirts. They had bright-colored bands around their waists and wore rough leggings and moccasins. Among these rough-and-ready men were fashionably dressed American businessmen and French and Spanish visitors from New Orleans.

Everywhere Jed heard people talking about the fur trade. The "fur fever" was in the air. Men talked excitedly about one trapping party that had just returned with $24,000 worth of beaver pelts. Just one year's work in the wilderness, they said.

The trappers discussed supplies and boats, and waterways. They talked about fierce beasts and Indians. Men who had been up the Missouri River pointed out that $2,000 worth of good trapping supplies could keep 20 trappers for a year. And each of these trappers might get at least $1,000 worth of furs.

Of course, Indians might wipe out your trapping party and you would not make a cent. You might even lose your life. But that was a chance you had to take if you wanted to make money in the fur trade. Trapping was a business for the strong, for men with grit and courage.

As Jed shouldered his way through one crowd, he heard a man saying, "Major Henry has taken a hundred men up the Missouri to trap beaver. Now his partner, General William Ashley, is going to send more men up the river in a few days. Wish I wasn't so old. I'd go along."

"Who are those fellows you're talking about—Henry and Ashley?" asked another man. "Do they know this fur business?"

"Who are Henry and Ashley?" echoed the first speaker. "You must be new around here or you wouldn't ask. Why, Major Andrew Henry was one of the men who started the Missouri Fur Company back in 1808. He led men up the Missouri to the three forks of the Madison, Jefferson, and Gallatin rivers. He was the first man to trap beaver west of the Rocky Mountains in the Snake River country."

As he spoke, the man waved his arms. He was clearly enjoying himself. "Major Henry," he continued, "has been in the lead mining business for the past ten years. But I guess he couldn't forget the mountains. He had to go back. Now, Ashley hasn't been up the

Missouri, but he is pretty important hereabouts. He is next to the governor in the State of Missouri, and a general in the militia."

Jed hurried away to find the office of General William H. Ashley. Perhaps the general would let him be one of the hundred to go up the Missouri!

A few minutes later, the young man from Ohio was standing before the man named Ashley. The general shook his head doubt-

fully as he looked at the slim, smooth-shaven youth with the eager eyes. "Jed," he said, "you certainly don't look twenty-three. Maybe it would help if you grew a beard and let your hair get longer."

"I can work as well as any man, General, hair or no hair. If you try me out for size, I will not let you down."

"Well, young man, I will sign you up with our company at $400 a year in spite of my doubts."

"Art Black! Come over here!" the general called out when Jed had signed up.

A husky man with yellow hair and beard walked over to Ashley's desk.

"Art, this is Jed Smith," said Ashley. "He's just signed up. Take charge of him and see that he has what he needs for the trip."

"Howdy, Jed," said Art. "Come along and meet some of the wild men who are going up the Missouri with you."

As Jed walked silently along the street, Art stole glances at him. "He looks awfully young to me," thought Art. "Wonder how he'll get along with those rough-and-ready wild men Ashley has? Well, he's tall and pretty husky and he might be tough if he got mad. The soft-spoken ones often are."

It was two days later that Hank Johnson and Joe Holt found out they couldn't push young Jed Smith around very long.

CHAPTER 3
Up the Missouri

Crowds cheered and dogs barked as General Ashley's keelboat, *Enterprise*, left St. Louis on May 8, 1822. Five days had passed since Jed's fight with Hank Johnson and Joe Holt. The always-cheerful Art Black had helped Jed forget the trouble with the two mountain men.

Now Jed stood on the deck of the keelboat and gazed up the river. At last, he was heading for the country he had dreamed of for so long! The seventy-five foot *Enterprise* was commanded by Cap-

tain Daniel Moore. The boat was heavily loaded with $10,000 worth of supplies for the trappers and goods to be traded to the Indians.

Among the supplies were rifles, powder, bullets, spare parts, and tools such as hatchets. There were also flint and steel, traps, knives, arrow points, fishhooks, files, needles, awls, and other small tools. For the Indians, there were blankets, kettles, cloth, ribbons, looking glasses, beads, and other trinkets.

On the keelboat, many of the crew of fifty were greenhorns who never had been more than a few miles out of town. There were clerks from St. Louis stores and offices. There were young men from rich families who had given up a life of ease to seek adventure in the wilderness.

But there also were twenty tough French boatmen who had the strength and grit to take the *Enterprise* up the wild Missouri River.

Then, too, there was Jim Clyman, a veteran mountain man. Jim was tall and slender. He had a gray beard and a long, curving mustache. His nose was like an eagle's beak, and his eyes were sharp and black under heavy gray brows. Jim knew the Missouri country through and through, and Captain Moore spent a lot of time asking him questions about the wilderness.

The wind being favorable, the *Enterprise* could use its big, square sail as it moved slowly up the Mississippi River. To help the riverboat on, men walked along the deck and pulled at the long oars, which stuck out on either side. But still it was a day and a night before the boat swung westward and entered the Missouri River.

More than the sail and the oars were needed to move the keelboat upstream now. So the French boatmen carried ashore the towline, which swung high from the mast of the boat.

Twenty men put the heavy, thousand-foot towline or cordelle over their shoulders and began to drag the *Enterprise* upstream against the strong current. The boatmen stumbled along the slippery bank, climbed over rocks and crashed through willows. Sometimes, they had to wade in water and mud up to their hips, but they sang loudly as they worked hour after hour. Nothing seemed to bother them.

"What are they singing about?" asked Jed.

"Don't rightly know," said Jim Clyman. "Sometimes I wonder if they know. But the tune kind o' puts ginger in a person, don't it?"

Jim leaned forward and watched the boatmen struggle. "This river is full o' trouble," he remarked. He pointed out snags of logs and drifted brushwood, which rose from the water like giant fingers. They forced the boat to go this way and that to get by them. Sawyers of sunken trees would suddenly leap out of the river like huge fish as the boat moved upstream.

"If one o' them sawyers or snags hits us," said Jim, "we'll be out o' business quick." Jed nodded his head then held his breath as great snags whirled by, clutched at the boat and slipped off.

Jim moved toward the bow. Jed followed him.

"The river, she is tricky," said one of the crew, smiling.

"The danged river don't know what she wants to do," Jim agreed. "Every time I go up the Missouri, the sandbars and whirlpools and banks are in a different place."

At night, the keelboat was pulled over to the bank and tied up. Then the men ate their meal of cornbread, beans, and pork and lay down to sleep on the riverbank. They slept hard each night.

Early in the morning, after their breakfast of cornbread, pork, and bitter coffee, they would have to go back to fighting the river. They knew that if they relaxed for a moment at the cordelle and the oars, the current would force the boat downstream.

One rainy, misty morning, Jim took a look at the river and told Captain Moore he'd better stay put that day. "Too risky trying to go up the Missouri when you can't see snags and sawyers of sunken trees," he said. "It's better to lose a day's travel than lose the boat."

Most of the time the crew could use both cordelle and oars to force the keelboat upstream. But when shallow places were reached, they had to use long poles. They set them on the bottom, rested the poles against their shoulders and pushed hour after hour. Other times, the men pulled the boat upstream by grabbing hold of branches of trees hanging over the riverbank.

Jed never got tired of looking at the country along the Missouri. He watched great white birds swim slowly ahead of the keelboat. Bright green birds such as he had never seen before chattered in the cottonwoods. Catbirds complained in the willows. Everything was beautiful in the daytime. But at night, humming clouds of mosquitoes settled on the men.

"Now, that's what I call a big one," said Art Black one night as he slapped a mosquito. "Felt like he was carrying a red-hot poker."

"These mosquitoes are a fair size," Jim Clyman agreed. "But wait till we get up in the mountains. Those mosquitoes are somethin' fierce. One night I killed two as big as a prairie chicken with its feathers plucked off. I roasted them mosquitoes and the boys didn't know the difference come mealtime."

Everybody laughed. They enjoyed Jim Clyman's tall tales.

Jim stretched his foot out toward the fire and pushed a log farther in. He had taught the greenhorns to build their fires Indian fashion. The ends of the logs, not the middle, were put in the blaze. Then as the logs burned, they were shoved into the fire.

"Seems like a lazy man's way of tending a fire," said a young man from St. Louis.

"Don't know about that," Jim answered. "But it works just as well as any. When we get into trappin' country you'll be too tired at night to cut up a log. You'll be glad you can just shove it in the fire with your foot."

A few days later, Jim took Jed and Art Black ashore to do some hunting. "I'm gettin' a little tired o' cornbread, beans, and salt pork," he said. "That's not fit food for mountain men. This should be country where there is fresh meat to be shot."

Jim was right. That day they shot an elk and a deer. The next day, they got a black bear, another deer, and several wild turkeys. Jim watched both Jed and Art bring down wild turkeys with their Hawken flintlock rifles.

"Pretty fair shootin'," he said. "A little more practice and you boys will be right good. You'll need to be good when we get into Blackfoot country."

The *Enterprise* was now nearing the Missouri-Nebraska border, more than 300 miles from St. Louis. The boat had got by hundreds of deadly snags and sawyers. But suddenly trouble struck from an unexpected direction. The mast of the fragile riverboat hit the overhanging limb of a tree, as the boat was moving slowly around a bend in the river.

Jim, Jed, and Art were just getting back from a hunting trip when they saw it happen. They saw the boat turn sideways to the swift current. They saw the water leap over the deck of the stricken vessel.

"She's a goner!" Art exclaimed.

In a few seconds the *Enterprise* was swept under. The boatmen all dropped the cordelle and splashed into the river to save what they could, while the men on the boat struggled ashore.

By God's grace, no members of the crew were lost. But all except a few dollars' worth of the supplies and trading goods had gone to the bottom of the Missouri.

Jed, Jim, and Art had run down to the riverbank. There they met the dripping, discouraged Captain Moore.

"I'll have to hurry back down to St. Louis and tell General Ashley what happened," said Moore.

"All right," Jim said. "I'll dry the men out and camp here till you get back."

"Don't think I'll be back!" said Moore. "I've had enough of this danged river to last me the rest of my life."

The captain, who had left a job as county clerk to seek adventure up the Missouri, had been wondering if he had been wise to come. Now he was sure he'd like life in St. Louis a lot better. But Jim wasn't discouraged at all.

"Do as you want, Captain," he said, shrugging his shoulders. He walked away and began building fires for the men. There was a lot of talk around the fires about going back. But in the end only three men decided to go down the river with Captain Moore and forget about the fur business. The rest grew cheerful again as soon as they had dried out. The thought of beaver pelts and adventure drew them on.

"I'll let you know what General Ashley wants to do," Moore said, just before he started back down the river to St. Louis in his hastily crafted canoe.

"I'm bettin' that the general will be right up here with more men," Jim answered. "He ain't one to quit once he's started out to do somethin'."

That night, around the fire, Jim talked about life on the upper Missouri. Jed put down his Bible to listen. Two young fellows from St. Louis were asking Jim questions about Indian fighting.

"I hear," said one, "that many Indians still use a bow and arrow. It shouldn't be hard for us to lick them with our rifles."

Jim shook his head. "I wouldn't say that," he said. "A three-foot sheepshorn bow can kill you at more than a hundred yards. An Indian can shoot eight or ten aimed arrows at you in thirty seconds. If you miss him the first shot, you're in for trouble because it takes you about thirty seconds to load and fire again. While you're doin' it, an Indian may fill you full of arrows."

"But I've heard it said that a mountain man can fire five shots in sixty seconds," remarked the other young man from St. Louis.

"Bosh!" said Jim. "It takes around twenty seconds to load a rifle. It takes another ten seconds to aim an' fire it if you want to be sure o' hittin' your target. As I said before, you better hit him first time or you may not get another chance."

Several of the greenhorns looked at Jim and smiled. "He's just trying to scare us with wild stories about the Indian's dangerous bow and arrow," they thought.

"I'll show you what I'm talkin' about."

Jim picked up his rifle and fired it toward the river. Then he said, "Art, you count slowly while I load. Drop your hand to your side and I'll start loadin'."

Art dropped his hand and began to count. Jim swung his powder horn around, pulled the stopper from it with his teeth, and quickly measured powder. Then he poured the powder into his rifle. Next, he wrapped a bullet in a small patch of greased buckskin and pushed it down the barrel with his ramrod. He then poured a little powder in the priming pan and was ready to fire.

Art Black had counted to sixteen when Jim put his rifle to his shoulder. "Well," said Jim, "I done better than I thought I'd do. But a man may not be as fast when arrows are flying and he's watching an Indian while tryin' to load."

The greenhorns looked at Jim Clyman with new respect. They had watched his swift movements, and they had to agree that few men could load a rifle faster than Jim had loaded his.

"You've proved your point, Jim," said Art Black. "This means I'm going to do some more practicing at loading and shooting before we get to Indian country."

"Jim," one of the men said, "I noticed that mountain men still use a Hawken flintlock rifle. Why don't they get the new rifle that uses a percussion cap to fire it? People are using them back East, I hear."

"A cap an' ball rifle is better than a flintlock in some ways," Jim agreed. "But it has its bad points."

"Why is it better? Just how does a rifle work anyway?"

Jim whirled around and looked at the speaker. "Where you been, son, that you don't know how a rifle works? Sorry, son. I forget that lots of lads don't spend most of their years in the mountains like I did," Jim went on when the other didn't answer. "If you ain't had the chance to learn, you'd better let me show you how rifles work."

As Jim looked at the greenhorn, he said "When you pull the trigger on a cap and ball rifle, the hammer falls an' hits the percussion cap. In the cap is some sort o' stuff that explodes when it gets hit hard. When it explodes, it touches off the powder in the barrel of the rifle an' away goes the bullet."

Jim picked up his Hawken flintlock and continued talking. "Now the flintlock don't work so easy. When you pull the trigger of a flintlock, this piece of flint in the hammer makes sparks when it falls on the priming pan. The sparks set off the powder in the priming pan an' then your rifle fires."

"You said the cap and ball rifle had its bad points," a greenhorn said. "Seems to me that a flintlock is pretty uncertain all the time. A man might get the powder in the priming pan wet, or he might lose the powder in the priming pan if he fell down."

"That's right," agreed Jim. "But what would happen if you lost the percussion caps for your cap and ball rifle when you were 1,500 miles from a trading post? You couldn't fire your rifle. You'd be in a right bad fix. But if you lose the flint for your flintlock rifle, you can always find another piece and fix up somethin' that will work."

Jim paused and looked around at the greenhorns. "I can see by the questions I been asked," he said, "that I better start givin' some of you lessons in handlin' a rifle. It'll be too late to learn when we get to Blackfoot country."

CHAPTER 4

In the Land of the Sioux

During the week, Jim kept a dozen or more greenhorns busy shooting their rifles and learning to load rapidly. "Remember," he said, "the big danger in an Indian attack is durin' the time when you're loadin' your rifle. That's when the Indian can get close enough to make sure of hittin' you with an arrow."

One evening, just at suppertime, a shout went up—a lookout had spotted a keelboat coming up the Missouri. There was great excitement. Everybody left his food to run down and greet the boat. It was Ashley with forty-five men and a new load of supplies and trading goods.

"Figured I'd be seein' you soon," said Jim Clyman as Ashley stepped from the boat.

"I'm not quitting now," Ashley replied, "Major Henry expects me to join him at the Yellowstone River, and I'm going to do it!"

Early the next morning, after the men had finished breakfast, the struggle against the Missouri began again. On up the river pushed the keelboat. It had been slow work before. Now it became slower. Grumbling began and it was heard more and more. The backbreaking toil at the cordelle, the oars, and the poles was getting to be too much for some of the men.

Wandering trappers had filled the minds of others with wild tales of bloodthirsty Indians and fierce grizzly bears. Some of the greenhorns forgot their brave talk in St. Louis about the things they would do in the wilderness. Men began to drop out and start back down the river.

One night, a heavy canoe going downstream pulled up beside the keelboat, and four bearded trappers stepped ashore to have coffee with Ashley and Jim Clyman.

"I'm Joe Beecher," said the tallest of the four men. "An' these here are my pals. We been playin' rough games with the Blackfeet for a year or so an' sure are ready to settle down in St. Louis for a spell. We wanta keep our scalps for a few more years."

"Too bad," said Ashley. "I'd like to have at least four more good men."

"We're meetin' Major Andrew Henry on the Yellowstone," said Jim. "He's a powerful good mountain man. But I suppose if you want to rest your bones in St. Louis, it's no use arguin' with you about goin' back to the Yellowstone."

"I didn't say I wouldn't go," Joe Beecher said. "What you offerin'?"

"Four hundred a year," replied Ashley.

"What do you say?" said Joe, turning to his friends.

"Guess maybe I ain't so anxious to see St. Louis as I thought. Probably be too quiet for me anyway," one of the men answered with a laugh.

"Me and Bill might as well get into this party," another said. So that night, four more men were added to the Ashley expedition.

"I knew we had 'em the minute they started talkin'," Jim Clyman said when he and Ashley were alone. "Real mountain men yell a lot about wantin' to get to St. Louis and take it easy. But they never do. Most of 'em won't quit bein' mountain men until some Blackfoot or grizzly makes 'em quit for good."

A day later, the keelboat reached the Platte River. It was that night that the greenhorns discovered they were in for something special. The old mountain men came running up with razors in their hands. "No man," they declared, "could go up above the Platte for the first time without having his beard and head shaved."

There was whooping and yelling as the veteran mountain men chased the greenhorns and shaved them. All they left Art Black was a small patch on top of his head.

Then they decided to catch Jed. "This here fellow don't play it fair," said Joe. "He shaves his beard and keeps his hair cut. Ain't much to work on here." Finally, they left a little line of hair running from the top of his head back to his neck.

This was the light side of the journey, and everybody made the most of it. Next morning, however, they knew that they would have to work harder than before and endure greater dangers.

Above the Platte, Ashley's men came to Fort Atkinson at old Council Bluffs. Here was where Lewis and Clark held a council with the chiefs of the Oto and Missouri tribes. Fort Atkinson was the last Army post on the Missouri River.

From that point on, Ashley's men were traveling through prairie country where the grass was several feet deep. Nothing but an endless forest of waving grass could be seen in every direction.

Several times during the trip, the men had been hit by sudden rainstorms. But Jim Clyman told the greenhorns that they hadn't really seen a bad storm yet. Then, one day, Jim eyed the sky and said to Jed, "Them clouds really look bad. We better pull the keelboat over to the bank and wait this storm out."

While the crew was working the boat toward the bank, lightning flickered and thunder rumbled. Then the wind howled down on them, bringing a blinding wall of water. Hailstones, as big as apples, pounded the men. One crash of thunder followed another for hours.

The next day, the battered men pushed on to the mouth of the Big Sioux River. The American Fur Company had a trading post there. Ashley's men only stayed at the trading post for a few hours. Then they struggled on up the Missouri, and soon they entered the country of the powerful Sioux Indians.

Up till then, Jed had not been impressed by the Indians he had seen. The Omahas and Poncas had been almost wiped out by sickness. They spent most of their time complaining about how poor they were and how much they needed food and powder.

The proud Sioux did no begging and asked no favors of the white men. They were still friendly, but they had to be handled carefully by white men who went through their country. A dozen of these Indians appeared suddenly along the bank of the Missouri, whooping and waving their guns and bows. Jim Clyman and Ashley went ashore to smoke the peace pipe with them.

Jed was near enough to the bank to study the Sioux closely. They were tall men, six feet or more in height. Several of them wore bonnets of eagle feathers and claws of grizzly bears around their necks. They were stripped to the waist and wore buckskin leggings. Their long hair was decorated with bones and feathers.

"You think Jim and the general are in danger?" one of the men asked Joe Beecher.

"That old hoss Jim Clyman knows how to talk with the Sioux," Joe replied. "The Sioux is mighty powerful fighters, as good as the Blackfeet. But so far the Sioux have been friendly with trappers, an' they ain't likely to start trouble without givin' some sign to you.

"Now the Blackfoot is a different kind of Indian. They are the orneriest Indians on earth. A Blackfoot is so mean he don't even like himself. We call 'em trouble from first to last."

It was hours before Jim and the general returned to the keelboat. "Them Sioux sure like to talk an' eat," said Jim. "I'm wore out. Guess I'm gettin' old for this sort o' thing."

"Did you do any trading with the Sioux?" asked Jed.

"No," Jim answered. "We just gave the chiefs some tobacco an' looking glasses. They gave us some advice."

"What advice?" asked Joe Beecher.

"They said to watch out for the Rees who have been raiding. The Rees have come in Sioux territory and attacked small parties o' trappers."

"Well, we'll soon find out about that," said Joe. "We should be at the Ree villages in a few more days."

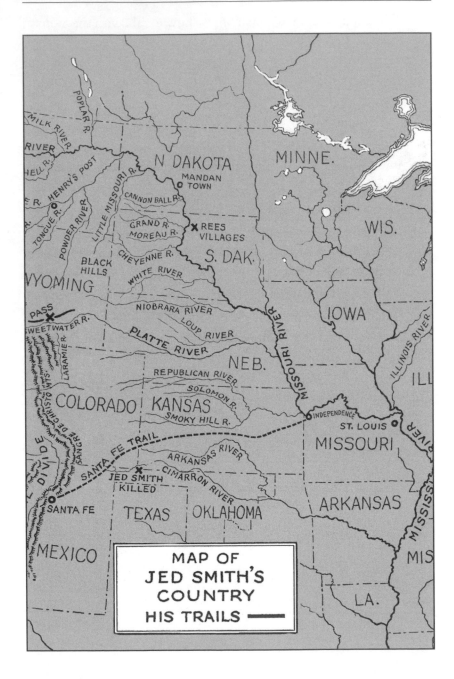

MAP OF
JED SMITH'S
COUNTRY
HIS TRAILS ▬▬▬

CHAPTER 5

On to the Yellowstone

Early in September, Ashley's party passed the mouth of the Grand River and reached the towns of the Rees. The two Ree towns were on the left side of the Missouri, about a quarter of a mile apart and three hundred yards from the river. The Rees lived in round huts made of poles, split timber, mud, and grass.

General Ashley took Jim Clyman, Joe Beecher, and Jed Smith ashore with him for a council with the Ree chiefs. As he walked toward the council lodge, Jed studied the Rees.

The warriors had colored their faces part green, part black. On their shoulders they wore buffalo skins. The hairy side was turned in and the skin side was decorated with paintings of animals and men.

There was a folded cloth between each warrior's legs. On his feet the warrior wore moccasins of deer and elk skin, while his legs were covered with hip-length leggings of antelope skin. Jed saw that the leggings were decorated with the hair of enemies killed in battle.

Jed seated himself with the others on the buffalo skin in the council lodge. Gray Eyes, the head chief, lighted the peace pipe with a coal from the fire. He pointed the pipe toward the sky, to each of the four quarters of the earth, and to the ground. Then he passed the pipe to the chief on his left. Each in turn took a puff.

Then Gray Eyes began to talk. Jim Clyman, the only trapper who understood the language of the Rees, repeated in English everything Gray Eyes said.

"Tell him," Ashley said, "that our hearts are good, too. Tell Gray Eyes that we also want peace and that we want to trade goods for horses."

Jim talked with Gray Eyes a few moments then turned back to Ashley. "Gray Eyes agrees to trade for horses. But first he wants us to eat with him."

Meat and corn were set before the guests. When all had eaten, Ashley brought out his trade goods and gave all the chiefs presents of looking glasses, cloth, tobacco, and blue beads.

For the next few days, Ashley's men traded for horses with the Rees. When they had collected fifty good horses, the keelboat pushed on up the Missouri while horse guards drove the herd along the banks.

General Ashley doubled the number of guards after Jim Clyman talked to him.

"Gray Eyes did a lot of talkin' about being friendly," Jim said. "But he might send some warriors to take back a few horses one of these days."

*****

Autumn had come to the upper Missouri and yellow leaves hung among the green. The rolling plains were yellow and dry.

Often in the golden distance, Jed would catch sight of swift-moving bands of antelope. The animals seemed to fly over the ground like low flying birds. Jim showed Jed how a rag waved on a ramrod would bring an antelope close enough for a sure shot. The curious beast just had to come close for a good look. Jim also pointed out a mule deer to Jed. Larger than the whitetail deer, it had ears almost like those of a donkey.

"When are we going to see a herd of buffalo?" asked Jed. "So far we've only seen a few old bulls that weren't worth bothering about."

"Wouldn't be surprised if we saw a big herd any day now," replied Jim.

As usual, Jim was right. The next evening, Jed suddenly felt the ground tremble. He looked quickly out across the plains. It seemed to him that all the buffalo in the world were there. The ground was covered with the shaggy animals. There seemed to be enough buffalo to eat all the grass in the whole country inside of a week.

"We won't try to pick off any tonight," said Jim. "Plenty of time to get a few fat cows tomorrow."

The next day, when another herd of buffalo came in sight, Jim said, "Now's the time." He and Jed got down from their horses and crawled forward cautiously to view the small herd.

"We ought to be able to get at least four of them," Jim said.

"Won't the others run after we fire the first time?" asked Jed.

"No," said Jim. "They won't pay no attention unless they catch our smell or see some quick movement of ours that disturbs 'em."

Jed and Jim were now less than a hundred yards from the herd. Jed looked admiringly at one huge bull. It was at least six feet high at the shoulder and looked as if it weighed 1700 pounds or more. The bull's hair was light at the forequarters and hump, and dark brown at the hindquarters and under the belly. "Now, Jed," said Jim. "Stretch out easy-like and aim for that cow nearest the big bull. Remember, shoot low—just above the chest is the spot."

Jed leveled his rifle and squeezed the trigger gently. There was a sharp crack, and the cow, taking a few steps, fell forward. Jim's rifle cracked a moment later. Jed saw that another cow was down. To his surprise, the herd kept on grazing as though nothing had happened.

"Load up quick," said Jim. "And be sure you don't scare 'em by wavin' your arm around. Take that cow on the far right and I'll get the one on the left."

The two rifles cracked at the same instant and two more cows fell. Then the herd suddenly broke into a run. The shaggy creatures looked clumsy, but Jed was surprised to see how fast they moved.

"Guess they saw somethin' that upset 'em," said Jim. "Well, never mind, Jed, we got plenty of meat anyhow. Now I'll show you how to do some butchering."

Jim set a cow on its belly with its legs spread wide on each side and then pulled out his butcher knife. He cut out the tongue first. Next, he made a cut down to the tail and spread the skin on each side of the cow. He made a small cut around the back of the neck, and the hump and hump ribs. As he worked, Jim began to talk.

"These hump ribs is good eatin'. You roast 'em over a fire. Now, this flesh between the backbone and the ribs is more good eatin'. Here's the side ribs, and now this is the lower belly fat. It's the best eatin' there is. No doubt about it, buffalo is the greatest meat animal on the face of the earth.

"Here's another thing that's good medicine for you," added Jim as he held up the liver. "Eatin' this helps keep a mountain man healthy. Fact is, buffalo meat will cure you o' just about anything."

With Jim helping him, Jed skinned and cut up the other cows. That night, Ashley's men were in high spirits. They could see buffalo hump cooking in kettles and cracked leg bones cooking by the fire. Ribs roasted on sticks slanted over the blaze.

Several hours later, the men were rolled snugly in their blankets near the fires. Jed could hear coyotes yipping nearby. Just as he drifted off to sleep he heard a wolf's lonely howl.

Sometime during the night, Jed woke up and noticed that one of the fires was blazing brightly. He saw that Jim Clyman and Joe Beecher were roasting a few more ribs. Mountain men never seemed to get enough of buffalo meat. Jed thought of joining them, but he went back to sleep.

For the next few days, Ashley worked every man he could use at the cordelle and the oars and poles. He was anxious to get to the Yellowstone for the fall hunting season. When at last the party reached the village of the Mandans, in what is now North Dakota, everybody was worn out.

The men hoped that Ashley would let them rest at the Mandan village for a few days. But the next day, the general pushed on up the Missouri.

Several miles up the river, Ashley halted his men and began dividing his party into two groups. He took half the men and all the horses and started overland for the Yellowstone. Jim, Jed, and Art Black were with him. The rest of the men were ordered to go on up the Missouri with the keelboat and join him at Henry's fort near the mouth of the Yellowstone.

On October 1, 1822, Ashley's party reached Henry's fort. The men fired guns and shouted questions about St. Louis, 1,780 miles down the Missouri. Jed was finally exploring the country he had dreamed about.

As they approached the fort, Jed began to think about his parents and his brothers and sisters and Dr. Simons. He felt ashamed because he hadn't thought of them much in the past months. Was he getting a little homesick all at once? No. He missed the people back home, but this was where he believed God wanted him to be.

While the men told stories and sang around the fires, Jed Smith read his Bible and then thought of the country beyond the Rocky Mountains.

CHAPTER 6
Jed Learns His Trade

General Ashley and Major Henry lost no time in making plans for the fall trapping. The unpredictable Blackfeet had been quiet for several months, and Henry's men already had several packs of fur ready to go to St. Louis. Ashley and Henry looked forward to a good trapping season on the beaver streams near the Missouri and Yellowstone rivers.

First, Ashley ordered Jim Clyman and Jed Smith to take a party of hunters up the Yellowstone and shoot a supply of meat for the fort. As they walked along the Yellowstone, Jed saw the yellow cliffs that give that river its name. Suddenly, Jim pointed to the left. Jed looked up and saw an animal with huge horns gazing down at the trappers from a nearby cliff.

"Rocky Mountain sheep are also called Bighorn sheep," said Jim.

The hunters saw many of these sheep leaping sure-footedly along the edges of cliffs. They also saw deer, rabbits, squirrels, and

other animals. Soon their rifles were cracking rapidly as they went about getting a supply of meat.

While Jim and Jed were out hunting, Major Henry sent one party of trappers to Powder River country. He took another party up the Missouri as far as the mouth of the Milk River. Ashley himself collected the fur packs on hand and started back down the Missouri for St. Louis.

When Jim and Jed returned from hunting, they, too, went up the Missouri to trap beaver. Winter was coming swiftly. Blackbirds fussed in the thickets and geese were flying south. Each day, the wind from the river was sharper. But Jed was dressed for any bad weather that might come.

He was dressed in fringed buckskin from his neck to his knees. The fringes could be pulled off and used to repair moccasins or leggings. From his knee to his ankle, Jed wore bright red woolen cloth. Many of the trappers wore cloth below their knees because they had to wade in water all the time. If they wore leather leggings, they would get smaller when they dried and nearly cripple the trapper. Woolen cloth also had the added benefit over leather of retaining its ability to keep the hunter warm even when it became wet. On his feet, Jed wore moccasins made of a single piece of buckskin. On his head, he wore a kerchief. When the weather got colder, he would wear a fur cap.

Fastened to Jed's belt were a butcher knife, a hatchet, two pistols, and a bag, which carried a trapper's "fixins" or "possibles." Among these "fixins" were flint and steel to use in making a fire, an awl for punching holes, and a piece of buckskin to repair moccasins. There were also fishhooks, needles, and other small odds and ends. Under Jed's right arm hung his powder horn and bullet pouch.

The trappers moved carefully along the creeks running into the Missouri looking for signs of beaver. As Jed, Jim, and the hunting party moved slowly upstream, Jim began to explain to the men the secrets of successful beaver trapping.

"It is wise to move upstream when entering unfamiliar hunting grounds, for if there are other trappers or Indians upstream, their sign will float downstream to you. Muddy water or a leaf floatin' downstream tells you somethin' is ahead," said Jim. "You don't want strange trappers or Indians around when you're trappin'. Trappers might steal your traps an' your pelts. Indians most likely will try to take your scalp."

Jim showed Jed a dam that beavers had built to make a pond. On the edge of the pond, they had built their house of small branches and mud. As the trappers waded upstream, Jed's feet became numb.

"One bad thing about this trappin'," said Jim, "is wadin' in cold water all the time. It makes a man's joints stiff. But you got to wade in water or the beaver will smell you and get out of the country."

Jim finally showed Jed a "slide" where a beaver had climbed the bank to get tender twigs. "Here's a good spot to set a trap," he said. They walked carefully around this spot and went up the stream several yards before they stepped out on the bank.

Jim took a steel trap with a five-foot chain on it. He spread the jaws of the trap wide, and set the trap's trigger. Then he cut a stout, dry pole. He carried the trap and pole to the spot he had chosen. He set the trap about five or six inches under the water and carried the chain out toward the center of the stream. Then, he drove the pole through a ring at the end of the chain and into the bed of the stream.

"This trap pole keeps the beaver from draggin' the trap up on the bank. If he can get on the bank, he'll gnaw his foot off and get away. You got to drown a beaver quick if you want to catch him," said Jim.

From his "possibles" bag, Jim took a small bottle. He held it up and said, "This stuff is beaver lure, which will bring a beaver hurryin' to your trap. And then, first thing he knows, he has a trap hangin' on his foot."

Jim dipped a small stick in the lure and fastened the stick

just above the jaws of the trap. He also tied a small dry stick to the trap with a narrow strip of leather. "This float stick is a good thing to have," Jim explained. "If a beaver happens to pull your trap pole loose and then drowns in deep water, the float stick shows where he is."

When the trap was ready, Jim splashed water on the bank to wash away any smell of humans. Then he and Jed waded on up the stream to find another spot for a trap. Each evening, Jim and Jed and the other hunters would set their traps. The next morning, they usually found that several beaver had been caught and drowned.

The trappers skinned the animals on the spot. Then they scraped the flesh and fat from the pelts and stretched them on willow frames to dry. A beaver weighed from thirty to sixty pounds, and the pelt a pound and a half to two pounds when dried. The pelts were pressed into "packs," each weighing around one hundred pounds.

Jed began to understand why trappers needed horses and mules when they were in the beaver country, for often there were heavy loads to carry over long distances.

The first beaver Jed caught was around three feet long. Its scaly, paddlelike tail was four inches wide and eighteen inches long. It was this tail, Jed learned, that made the beaver such a good swimmer. The young trapper from Ohio also discovered that the tail was very good eating. All one had to do was burn off the scaly skin and boil it.

Jed examined his first beaver with great interest. The hump-backed creature had a squirrel-shaped head and small ears. Its fore-feet were a lot like human hands, he thought, except that they were webbed and had long digging claws. The silky fur was a rich, dark brown—all except the tail, which was gray.

All the time they were trapping, Jim kept a sharp lookout for Indians. He tried to teach Jed to be watchful, too.

"Keep in mind, Jed," he said, "that we are in Blackfoot country. A man who don't keep his eyes and ears open don't live long when he's hunting on another man's land. When you move upstream, keep watchin' the water for a sign of somethin' ahead of you.

"When you follow a trail, watch for a blade of grass that's pressed down or a turned leaf. If you spot wild animals that are runnin', or birds actin' excited, look sharp for Blackfeet. Your eyes can tell you a lot if you use 'em right."

"Now, here's somethin' interestin'," said Jim a few moments later. "What do you make o' that?"

"I see a hare sitting under that bush," said Jed proudly.

"Right. Was that hare scared?" asked Jim.

"How in the world could you tell if he were scared?" replied Jed.

"Look right over there," said Jim. "See those tracks. They are so far away from the others that you know that the hare made a leap. Somethin' scared it. What scared it?"

Jed shook his head sadly. He wasn't feeling proud any longer.

"Well," said Jim, as he tried to keep from laughing. "There's no other tracks around so it must of been an eagle or a hawk. This shows what I been sayin' about keepin' your eyes open in the woods," said Jim, as he walked on down the trail.

"When you're travelin' with a horse or a mule," Jim said later, "keep an eye on 'em. Horses an' mules don't like the smell o' Indians. They'll let you know quick if there are any Indians around. Mules are even better than horses at spottin' Indians."

Each day Jed found another reason why Jim Clyman had been able to spend years in the Indian country and had lived to tell about it. He seemed to know where every rock, tree, and bush in the region was. His sharp eyes never missed a thing. He would lie as motionless as a stone and study the trail for hours.

Jim could be as patient as a mountain lion waiting for a deer. When he slept, he seemed to have one ear cocked for any sound. When he woke up, he was wide-awake in a second. Jed couldn't admire and respect his wilderness teacher enough, although he knew that the Lord was ultimately the One who was empowering and preserving his friend.

"That's how I've got to learn to be," Jed told himself. "If I want to keep on trapping and exploring in Indian country, I've got to learn all the Indians' tricks."

The trappers didn't stay long in any one spot, for they knew better than to overhunt any one pack of beavers. After they had trapped in one creek a few days, the men moved to another and then still another. By winter, they had reached the mouth of the Musselshell River. It was now time to build shacks and settle down.

The weather had turned bitterly cold. The ground was hard as stone. The Missouri froze from bank to bank. But in their camp the trappers were snug. They had plenty of meat, for they had shot deer and squirrels and mountain sheep.

One day, they had caught sight of hundreds of buffalo crossing the Missouri on the ice. For the next few days the men had shot as many fat cows as they wanted. Now every night, humps boiled in the kettles and ribs roasted on sticks slanted over the fire.

"A buffalo is not only the best eatin'," said Jim Clyman. "He's mighty useful in lots of ways. The hair on his head is thick and springy. Makes a good pillow if you like that sort of thing. The buffalo's fur is soft as lamb's wool," he added, "and it makes a robe that don't weigh a man down but keeps him plenty warm."

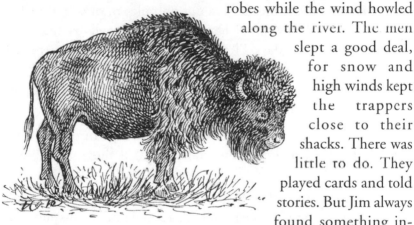

Jed often thought of Jim's words as he settled down in his robes while the wind howled along the river. The men slept a good deal, for snow and high winds kept the trappers close to their shacks. There was little to do. They played cards and told stories. But Jim always found something interesting to tell about the creatures of the wilds.

"A grizzly," he said one night, "is one ornery animal. But there is one other animal that is more ornery. That's the wolverine. If I ever find that a wolverine's been fooling around my trap line, I get out of the country. No use tryin' to fight him. A wolverine is part devil and part grizzly."

"What's a wolverine look like, Jim?" asked Jed.

"Like a small bear with long, shaggy fur and a short bushy tail. Not countin' the tail, a wolverine may be about three feet long. He don't weigh over forty pounds, but he is the meanest thing in the world, pound for pound. Even grizzlies let wolverines alone."

"A Canadian trapper told me," said one of the old mountain men, "that he once shot fifty bullets into a wolverine. The wolverine just spit the bullets back at him."

"Spit them back!" laughed Art Black. "That tale sounds a little wild to me, Bill."

"Maybe Bill's story is a little wild," replied Jim Clyman. "But any trapper who has had to run into a wolverine soon gets to thinking that they can do anything. I only hope there's no wolverines around these parts," Jim added.

One cold day, Jed watched Jim cut strips of buffalo meat an inch thick and then spread them out on poles to dry. "I'm makin' more jerky," explained Jim. "The wind and sun will dry this batch of meat in about five days. I'll put a smoky fire under another batch an' it'll dry in three days. Wood smoke makes a real sweet jerky."

"How do you make the pemmican I've heard the trappers talking about?" asked Jed.

"Well," said Jim. "It takes jerky to make pemmican. Here's some jerky Bill dried the other day. Now, I'll show you how he did it."

With a sharp knife, Jed cut all the tough parts from a pile of jerky. Then he pounded the meat with a stone until it was almost as fine as flour. Next, he packed the powder loosely in a large rawhide bag and poured melted fat over it.

"Here's your pemmican," said Jim. "It'll keep sweet in this bag for years. Pemmican is the best food there is when you're traveling fast and hard. It sticks to a man's ribs, gives him a lot of strength. Of course," Jim added, "berry pemmican is the best eating of all, but trappers usually don't bother with making it. The Indian squaws make it by pounding dried wild cherries or some other fruit into the jerky."

Spring came slowly to the upper Missouri country. But one morning, Jed woke to hear a welcome sound. It was running water.

The ice in the brook had melted! Within a few weeks, high water was rolling down the Missouri. Huge cakes of ice crashed together with a roar that could be heard for miles.

The men were impatient to be gone. The snow was still on the ground in places when Jed and Jim led their trapping party back down the Missouri to Henry's fort.

Only a small party of trappers was there to greet them. Ashley, they were told, was in St. Louis. He promised to bring another party of trappers to the Yellowstone in June or July. In the meantime, Henry had gone on up the Missouri to trap beaver.

Jim Clyman shook his head at this news. "I got a feeling Major Henry is in for trouble," he said. "The Blackfeet have been quiet too long, and the major is right in the middle of Blackfoot country."

Jim's fears were only too right. A few days later, Major Henry and a dozen exhausted trappers rode into the fort. Others came in during the next three days. Several of the men were wounded, and ten were missing. Only a few packhorses had been saved.

The Blackfeet had attacked the major's camp near the Great Falls of the Missouri. The trappers had saved themselves only by making a swift retreat. Major Henry had killed one Blackfoot in a hand-to-hand fight but had received a wound in the arm.

"I'm not retreating any farther," Henry said as Jim worked on his arm. "We'll hang on here and wait for General Ashley. He was supposed to have left St. Louis early in March with two keelboats."

"It might be a good idea to send someone down the river to meet him and hurry him along," said Jim.

Henry agreed. "You know this country better than any man here. How about you going?" he asked.

"All right, Major, if I can take Jed Smith with me," replied Jim. "That boy is getting to be a right good mountain man, and it's time I showed him more of this country."

A day later, Jim and Jed were on their way, mounted on two of the best horses that were left. They would try to hit the Missouri River somewhere near the mouth of the Cheyenne.

"I figure we oughta meet Ashley about there," said Jim, as he pointed to a spot on a crude map that he had made by scratching on the ground with a stick.

CHAPTER 7
Fight with the Rees

Jim Clyman had no way of knowing when Ashley would get to the Cheyenne. But the mountain man's judgment was so good that what he guessed was better than what other men thought they knew. Just below the mouth of the Cheyenne, Jim and Jed came upon Ashley's party. Two keelboats were slowly moving up the Missouri.

Jim wasted no time talking to Ashley's men. He quickly took the general aside and gave him the bad news from Major Henry. Ashley, too, had bad news to report.

Wandering trappers had told him the Rees were in an ugly frame of mind. One band of Rees had entered Sioux territory and robbed a party of fur traders. They had then attacked Fort Recovery, the trading post of the Missouri Fur Company near the White River. Several Indians had been wounded in that fight. Two had been killed, one of them, a chief's son.

Now, it was reported, the Rees were planning to leave their towns and join the Mandans. Together they meant to fight any trapping party that tried to go up the Missouri to the Yellowstone River.

"We're in a bad fix," said Jim. "We can't go overland to the Yellowstone unless we get packhorses. The Rees are the only Indians hereabouts that have horses. We'll just have to keep on going and take a chance on their staying friendly with us."

"That is what I've been thinking," said Ashley. "The Rees have the horses and they control the river. We'll have to talk peace with them."

On the afternoon of May 30, the two keelboats, rounding a bend of the Missouri, approached the Ree villages. Jim Clyman shook his head as he looked around him. The Rees had built a palisade of logs around their villages. Pointing it out to Ashley, Jim said, "This ain't good. Looks like they're getting ready to start trouble."

Slowly they advanced. When they were within forty yards of the lower Ree village, Jim began to signal to the Rees. "The white men are peaceful! They want to trade for horses!"

Three Indians, who appeared to be chiefs, came out in answer to the signals. Ashley, with Jim and Jed, went ashore to meet them. Silently, all squatted on the sandy beach. From the keelboats and from the roofs of huts, hundreds of eyes watched them.

When the peace pipe had been puffed, Jim Clyman addressed the Ree chiefs. He spoke in Ashley's name. His chief's heart was good, he said, and he would speak straight words. He was sad when he heard that there had been trouble at Fort Recovery. He was sorry that the son of a Ree chief had been killed. He hoped that the Rees would not be angry with all white men because of what had happened. Ashley was not a man with a weak heart, he pointed out. He was a big chief in his own country.

On his keelboats were a hundred men who could shoot straight. If there was trouble, many Rees would die. That would not be right because the white chief wanted peace. He had passed this way a year ago and had traded peacefully with the Rees. He wanted to trade again for horses to take to his friends on the Yellowstone River.

The Rees listened in silence. When Jim had finished, they got up and walked a little distance away to hold a council. For many minutes, they stood talking together.

As he waited, Jed could feel sweat running down his ribs. He glanced at Jim to see if he were worried. But the old mountain man seemed to be dozing. Ashley was nervously fingering his belt, but he said nothing.

At last, the Indians returned. The chiefs were sorry, they said, for what had happened down the Missouri near the White River. But that was long ago and they were no longer angry. They knew that the big white chief spoke straight words. They would speak straight words too. They had many good horses and were willing to trade with the white men.

Ashley openly showed his pleasure. He presented rich gifts of cloth and beads. The next day, Jim told the chiefs that the white men would return to trade for horses.

When Ashley, Jim, and Jed came back to the *Yellowstone*, the crew cheered loudly. Several of the St. Louis greenhorns had been nervous while the talk was going on. They had looked at the Ree warriors crowding the roofs of huts and had wished themselves back in St. Louis. Now that the danger seemed to be over, they were brave again.

"Those Rees don't know how lucky they were not starting a fight! We could have wiped them out easily if they had wanted trouble!" said one young fellow.

"Yes," said another, "and wait till we join Henry at the Yellowstone. Then we'll be so strong that no Indian tribe in the whole Missouri country will risk picking a fight with us!"

Jim Clyman watched the greenhorns. "The foolish boys will talk an' boast 'cause they don't know better. As for me, I'll just keep quiet and see that my rifle is in good shape. I can smell trouble comin'. If any of you be praying men, I suggest that you start now."

The closing words of Jim Clyman hit the nervous trapper named Jed rather hard, for he had let himself get out of the habit of daily prayer and Bible reading. Jed was convicted by the Holy Spirit to get back to the vital exercise of prayer as he remembered the parting words of Dr. Simons who said, "Don't give up your faith."

For the next day and a half, the Rees and the trappers argued over the value of each shaggy Indian pony brought on the beach.

The Rees drove a hard bargain, and it troubled the desperate trappers that the Indians would take only powder and bullets in exchange. "I don't like that at all," Jim Clyman grumbled. "We are going to get them bullets shot back at us mighty soon."

By the evening of June 1, enough horses had been bought. Jim, Jed, and forty of the more dependable men were to take the animals cross-country to the Yellowstone area. For one more night, however, the men would have to stay on the beach. To keep the herd together, the trappers put a rawhide hobble around the front legs of each horse. With a hobble on, the horses couldn't get very far.

Jim Clyman looked over the camp on the beach and then studied the Ree palisade. It was only about a hundred yards away. Jim did not like this. He went to the keelboat to talk to Ashley.

"I think we are making a mistake camping on the beach tonight with those horses," Jim said. "If the Rees start a fight, we will be pushed into the river and we'll lose most of the horses."

Ashley, however, was not expecting a fight.

Jim shrugged his shoulders. There was nothing for him to do but go back to the beach and keep on guard. He called Jed to him.

"Ashley is not expecting any trouble, but I am," he said. "Go among the men and tell 'em to stay awake tonight and keep their rifles handy. I don't see how we can save our horses if the Rees attack. But we sure can make it rough for them."

That night, drums boomed in the villages. The Rees were holding a feast. The singing of the warriors and squaws could be clearly heard by the white men seated around fires on the beach. They didn't mind the singing. It was the drums that bothered them. Jim Clyman moved watchfully about the camp, quieting the men.

It was hours before the drums were silent, and then he had new trouble on his hands. A sudden storm swept down upon them. Rain lashed the beach, lightning forked in the sky, and thunder grumbled over the plains. The excited horses were so badly frightened that Jim had to send more guards out to calm them.

Around three o'clock, a dripping horse guard came to Jim Clyman. "One of the men just came back from the Ree villages. He thinks the Rees are getting ready to attack us." Jim sent the horse guard to warn Ashley to get ready for trouble. Then he walked down the line of men on the beach and checked up on them. By now, the rain had about stopped but there were no stars out and the night was black.

Jed crouched behind a log and peered into the darkness. He found the silence more disturbing than the Ree drums. The rain stopped completely as dawn came slowly along the Missouri. The men relaxed a little. The horse herd was quiet. Maybe there was not going to be an attack after all.

Suddenly, an owl hooted on the left of the Ree palisade. This hoot was answered on the right.

"They're goin' to attack!" shouted Jim Clyman.

Jim's voice was answered by a puff of smoke from the Ree palisade and the crack of a rifle. Then the whole length of the palisade spouted smoke and flame as the Ree rifles went into action. The horses plunged around in their hobbles. Several horses screamed and fell in the sand.

One trapper fell across a log and another dropped his rifle and grabbed his shoulder. Jim Clyman moved swiftly along the line of men. He paused behind one greenhorn who had been firing wildly at the palisade.

"Take it easy, Hoss!" shouted Jim. "We got no powder an' lead to waste blowin' holes in the air. Wait till you see somethin' to shoot at. Then squeeze the trigger gentle-like."

The man looked at Jim's calm face. He relaxed and began to load his rifle. His hands no longer trembled. He rested his rifle on the log in front of him and watched the puffs of smoke along the palisade. The man next to him fired at the palisade and yelled wildly. "Take it easy, Hoss!" he shouted at the man. "Don't go blowin' holes in the air. Wait till you got something to shoot at!"

When the attack started, Jed Smith had quickly turned his attention to the horses. More were falling every minute and Jed saw they had to be set loose, or else the Rees would wipe out the whole herd. He called to three men to help him cut the hobbles. He hoped to drive the excited animals into the river and make them swim to safety.

But the Ree rifles kept on cracking and more and more horses went down screaming and kicking. Two of the men Jed had called to help him had been killed almost at once and the third was wounded. It was hopeless. The horses couldn't be saved.

When Jed went back to the line and started firing, everybody was amazed. They couldn't believe he hadn't been hit. Bullets had kicked up sand all around him as he struggled to free the horses.

Meantime, Ashley had been trying to get the men on the keelboats to help those on the beach, but with no success. Most of the crew were French boatmen who had no desire to fight Rees. They were willing to work cheerfully day after day at the cordelle. But Indian fighting was not their business, and they told Ashley so.

At last, after much argument, he did get a few men to bring a boat ashore to save those on the beach.

"The men want to stay here and finish the job!" yelled Jim Clyman, when Ashley brought up the boat. "They'll do it, too, if you get some help!"

By this time the fighters were no longer scared greenhorns. They had seen their friends killed and they wanted to fight back.

"Give us a chance to wipe out those villages!" they shouted. But Ashley was helpless. The keelboat crews would not help them. The only thing to do was to get the men out before all of them were killed.

But only a few men could get into the boat Ashley had brought ashore. The rest splashed into the Missouri and swam for the keelboats. Two wounded men were drowned trying to reach the boats. The others, exhausted and dripping, were hauled aboard by the crewmen. A few horses were taken across the river to safety. In all, twelve men had been lost and ten wounded.

That night, Ashley called his men together and urged them to make one more effort to pass the Ree villages. "If we stay out in the middle of the river," he said, "we should get by without too much trouble."

But only Jim, Jed, and a half dozen others were willing to try to pass the villages the next day. The men had had enough of Indian fighting.

"Can't say that I blame these youngins and the boatmen for not wanting to try again," said Jim. "They see that Ashley made a bad mistake putting the horses on the beach. He let the Rees fool him with peace talk. The general is brave enough. But he don't know much about Indians and Indian fighting."

CHAPTER 8

Jed Takes a Message to Major Henry

The day after the fight with the Rees, General Ashley called another meeting of his men. He was very angry, but he had taken time to think things over.

"I agree that it is no use to try to go past the Ree village at this time," he said. "So I have decided to move back down the Missouri to the mouth of the Cheyenne River. "I shall send a message to Major Henry and ask him to join us. We can then plan our next move. But it will be a dangerous trip to Henry's fort near the Yellowstone. I must ask for a volunteer." Jed stepped forward quickly and Jim Clyman followed.

"You're my man, Jed," said Ashley. He was smiling for the first time in two days.

"General," said Jim, "Jed will get to Henry if anyone can. But I've been over that country. I'm thinking that two men oughta make this trip. They can sorta look after each other in case of trouble. It's more than two hundred miles to the Yellowstone and the country is likely to be stiff with Indians."

"You're right, Jim," Ashley said. "But I can't spare both of you."

"My General, I am ready to go." The speaker was Pierre, a French-Canadian trapper who had joined Ashley at Fort Recovery. Pierre grinned broadly as he stepped over beside Jed and said, "I think we get to Henry easy. I can smell Indians two, three miles away."

"Fine," said Ashley. "How soon can you men start?"

"We'll round up two horses and start tonight," replied Jed.

At dark Jed and Pierre mounted their shaggy Indian horses and quietly started out. They had no guide except the North Star. But it was enough. They urged their little horses into a jog trot and made good time. They were traveling light. Each man carried a rifle, a pistol, and a butcher knife. For food, they had cornbread and dried meat.

Dawn found the travelers by the Grand River in territory familiar to both. Pointing to a strip of timber off to the right, Pierre asked, "We go there, hide in trees and rest horses a little?"

"Yes," said Jed. "I think we all need a little rest."

Near the Grand River, Jed and Pierre tied their horses to a tree and then stretched out in the grass. It was not safe to make a fire, so they ate a cold breakfast. "Indians smell smoke of fire, two, three miles," Pierre remarked.

When they had finished eating, Jed decided to rest an hour or so, for both he and Pierre were badly in need of sleep. "We won't unsaddle the horses, though, since we will be leaving soon," Jed said.

It was probably leaving the horses saddled that saved the lives of Jed and Pierre.

It seemed to Jed that he had been sleeping just a few minutes when the neighing of the horses awoke him. He sprang to his feet and grabbed his rifle. Pierre jumped up, too. "Where is the sun?" he asked excitedly. "She is not in the east."

Jed swung around and saw the sun dipping low in the west. Then he realized that he had slept all day. The fight with the Rees and the all-night ride had worn them out. But what had disturbed the horses? What was wrong?

Jed and Pierre crouched down, moved to the edge of the trees, and looked to the east. A band of at least twenty-five mounted Indians was riding down a steep bluff into the valley. The warriors were not more than half a mile away. From the valley they spread out and began riding cautiously toward the trees where Jed and Pierre crouched.

"They know we're here," said Jed. "But they're taking their time until they find out how strong we are. Let's get out before they find that there are just two of us."

Within a few seconds, Jed and Pierre were galloping down the valley. A mile down the valley they swung to the right and plunged into the river. They heard the rising yells of the warriors as they splashed through the water.

Jed felt that their chances of escaping were good. Their horses had been resting all day while the Indians' horses had been traveling for many hours. "If we gain on the Indians while it is still light," thought Jed, "we can get away from them tonight."

All through the evening Jed and Pierre pushed their horses. Only when the stars came out did they stop to let the animals rest. Pierre dropped to the ground and listened for many seconds.

"I hear no thing," he said. "Indians three, four miles away, I think."

"Well," said Jed, "they've given us quite a chase, and our horses are almost worn out. We better move on. But let's lead the horses a while and give them a little more rest while we can."

But a few minutes later, Pierre stopped, raised his head, and sniffed.

"I smell smoke," he said. "Maybe Rees. We are in trouble, I think."

"Stay here with the horses," said Jed, and picking up his rifle, he moved carefully down the valley. He finally worked his way around the base of a bluff on the right. About a hundred yards ahead, he saw the dull glow of a fire in among some cottonwoods.

He began crawling toward the fire. As he crawled, he carefully picked every stick out of his way for fear it might snap. After several minutes of this slow crawling, Jed peered through a clump of bushes and saw a Ree sitting near the fire.

The Ree's chin was resting on his chest and he seemed ready to fall asleep at any moment. Another Ree was stretched out on the ground nearby. Jed could hear horses stamping and blowing in the darkness.

It was a hateful thought to Jed, but he knew he had to kill these two Indians. Their camp was too near the trail to risk trying to slip by them. And a bluff to the right was too steep to climb in the darkness. Furthermore, he and Pierre needed the horses of those two Rees. The band of warriors behind them was getting closer every minute.

Should he crawl back and tell Pierre about the Rees? No, Jed decided, there was no time. Every second counted. He carefully checked the priming of his rifle and pistol. Then he put his pistol near him and stretched out on the ground. He aimed at the Ree sitting near the fire with his rifle and pulled the trigger. Then grabbing his pistol, he leaped forward.

The first Ree had fallen across the fire. As Jed charged into the camp, the other Ree reached for his rifle. But Jed's pistol cracked too fast. Before the Indian could pull his trigger, he, too, lay dead. By the time Pierre arrived, Jed was moving toward the Ree horses.

"What you do?" he called out. "Indians shoot at you?" Then he saw the two Indians on the ground.

"They never had a chance," said Jed. "I hated doing it, but we couldn't have got by them, and we need their horses."

"You hated doing it? I no understand," said Pierre. "Indians are for shooting at. They shoot at us. It is the way of things out here."

"Well, I don't have the time to argue with you here," replied Jed. "Go get their horses while I collect our saddles."

"First, I'll help you take the scalps," said Pierre as he whipped out his knife and grinned happily.

"No!" said Jed angrily. "It is bad enough to kill! But the taking of scalps makes us worse than the people we like to call savages!"

"But the mountain men, they always take scalps!" said Pierre, in a surprised tone.

"No," said Jed grimly. Pierre stared at him several moments. Then he walked toward the Indians' horses. Jed suddenly realized that his right hand was gripping his knife. Would he have used the knife on Pierre? He shook his head. He wondered if he were not already becoming a savage.

Six hours later, the men moved downhill to a bullberry thicket and made camp. Jed was very troubled in mind and spirit. He staked out the horses to graze and then told his heartless companion to get some sleep. Before Jed closed his tear-stained eyes to sleep, he cried out in his spirit to the Lord. He prayed, "Lord, your hand is heavy upon me, and so I seek your face to repent of my sin of killing men made in your image without just cause. Forgive your servant for his sinful actions toward two poor creatures who were standing in need of the love of Christ. Help me to be guided more by love than by fear and to turn from my foolish fits of anger, which never do advance your holy purposes. Lead me, Father, from the shedding of innocent blood to the life of peace that is founded upon the sure mercies of Jesus Christ. Cleanse my soul, dear God, for Jesus' sake. Amen"

When the shadows began to darken the valley, Jed and Pierre started out again. It was about midnight when they reached the forks of the Grand River.

"I'm not sure which fork of the Grand is best for fast traveling," said Jed. "Let's leave the river for good and strike out across the prairie. We can keep our course by watching the North Star."

They jogged out across the prairie. But within an hour, they were in trouble. The sky grew dark, rain began to fall, and they no longer could guide themselves by the North Star. For a while they kept on, but finally the rain began falling too heavily.

"We get lost," said Pierre. "We wander in circles in storm. Better stop."

"You are right," replied Jed. "We'll stake out our horses right here and wait till morning."

Throughout that night, Jed and Pierre huddled together with their blankets over their heads. Rain was still falling heavily in the morning. It was no use trying to make a fire. So they mounted their dripping horses and chewed on cornbread and jerky as they rode across the dreary land.

The plain had become a dreary swamp in the heavy rain, and the horses' hooves sank deeply into the ground. Jed and Pierre had to dismount several times and walk to give the animals a rest. But they couldn't walk for long. The mud was too hard on them. It sucked at their moccasins and nearly pulled them from their feet.

The rain was still falling at nighttime, and again no fire could be made. Again they huddled under wet blankets. But when morning came, the rain had stopped. A warm sun cheered the men up. They ate and rode on. About noon, they climbed a hill and looked westward. Before them was the valley of the Little Missouri River.

"I think we do some hunting soon," remarked Pierre. That afternoon, he shot a sheep. A few hours later, they made camp. The men roasted generous pieces of meat over a fire while their horses grazed contentedly on the thick green grass. In between bites of lamb meat, the curious Frenchmen asked Jed, "Why do you talk of this God of yours so much?"

"For the same reason that you determine not to speak of Him—because it gives me pleasure. When the good Lord, who made you and all things, gets a hold of your heart, you can no more pretend that He doesn't exist than a fish can pretend he doesn't need water," Jed replied.

"I no understand," responded Pierre.

"Some day soon, my lost friend, I hope and pray that you will," said Jed soberly.

Early the next morning, Jed and Pierre crossed the Little Missouri and struck out in a northwestward direction. Soon, they were crossing creeks that were flowing north.

"We are getting near the Yellowstone," said Jed. "That river is north of us and these creeks must be flowing into it. It won't be long now before we get to Henry."

Two days later, they came to a small stream, which they followed down to the Yellowstone River.

"Plenty good hunting here," said Pierre.

"Plenty of Indians, too," replied Jed. "We'd better travel only at night and hide out during the day. We'll do no hunting or making of fires in this country."

After two days of night travel, they reached the place where the wide, slow moving Yellowstone meets the Missouri. An hour later, Jed and Pierre were at Henry's fort on the south bank of the Missouri four miles from the Yellowstone.

The gates swung open to receive the travelers. Trappers swarmed around them. "Where's Ashley?" everybody wanted to know. "When's he coming up here?"

Jed left Pierre to tell the story of their adventures and pushed through the crowd to find Major Henry. In his cabin, the major listened quietly to the story of the fight with the Rees.

"So Ashley is in trouble, too!" Henry exclaimed. "Seems like all of us have a full share of hard times." The major got up and paced the floor. Suddenly he stopped short.

"It's no use moaning about tough times," he said. "I've got to act. I'll leave twenty men here and take the rest down the Missouri in my keelboat. We'll start tomorrow. You and Pierre will come with me. Now I guess you could stand something to eat and a cup of strong drink."

"I'd like something to eat," replied Jed. "But I don't need a strong drink."

"You've been in these mountains over a year and you still drink water," said Henry, laughing. "Well, you don't seem to need anything stronger to keep you going, young fellow. Come along and try some hump ribs."

CHAPTER 9
Ashley's New Idea

The next morning, Major Henry and his men started down the Missouri to join Ashley near the Cheyenne. The melting snows in the mountains were pouring water into the Missouri, and the swift current took the keelboat rapidly downstream.

Jed recalled the struggles with oars, poles, and the cordelle on the upward journey. This, he decided, was a much more pleasant way to travel on the Missouri. The men had little to do but eat, sleep, smoke their pipes, and tell tall stories. Jed, however, took advantage of the quiet time to catch up on his study of God's Word, as well as history and geography.

Near the end of June, the keelboat drifted past the mouth of the noisy Cannonball River. "We're getting near the Ree villages," said Art Black. "Wonder if they will be waiting to give us a hot welcome."

"We'll be ready if they want to fight," remarked Henry.

Two days later, the boat moved around a right-hand bend of the Missouri and swept by the Ree villages. The men crouched in the boat and held their rifles ready, but on the riverbank children and barking dogs were racing back and forth. Indian warriors ran along the bank waving buffalo robes.

"The Rees are telling us that they are peaceful and want to do some trading," said Henry. "But we aren't stopping to find out."

The keelboat drifted swiftly down the river and left the villages far behind. The next afternoon, Major Henry's men reached Ashley's camp near the mouth of the Cheyenne.

Huge fires blazed that night as the trappers stretched out on the ground and talked of past years on the upper Missouri River. Old mountain men kept the greenhorns open-mouthed with their tales. They spoke of Indians and bears and dangers and narrow escapes.

They couldn't say enough about John Colter, the first of the mountain men. Colter had been with Lewis and Clark on their trip to the mouth of the Columbia River and back. Colter and his men dared to trap beaver in the land of the cunning Blackfeet. After several escapes, Colter finally was caught by them.

Colter hoped that the Blackfeet would kill him quickly. After discussing what to do with him, the Indians decided to have some sport with the mountain man. They stripped him and even took his moccasins. Then they untied his hands and told him to start running. Colter ran and the whole band of Blackfeet took out after him, whooping and waving their lances.

Colter was running for his life, and he really ran. He soon left all but three of the Blackfeet far behind. Slowly but surely, one of these three warriors closed in on the tired man. His effort to run faster caused blood to pour from his nose.

Wildly, he looked over his shoulder and saw the Blackfoot starting to throw his lance. Colter crouched and whirled around. The warrior tried to check his throw, stumbled and fell on one knee. Before he could recover, Colter leaped on him and killed him with his own lance. Then he raced away before the other Blackfeet could overtake him.

The angered warriors wanted more than ever to catch and kill this tough mountain man. He was beginning to stumble from weariness as blood kept pouring from his nose. Suddenly, he came upon a small stream. In he plunged and hid under a pile of driftwood. The cold water checked the flow of blood from his nose.

The Blackfeet ran up and down the stream for an hour and finally went back to their camp.

The exhausted, half-frozen mountain man crawled out on the bank and went to sleep. Hours later, he woke up and began his hundred mile trip from the Jefferson River country to Lisa's Fort near the Big Horn and Yellowstone rivers.

Colter wandered for days, eating berries and anything else he could find. The weary man finally reached Lisa's Fort and told the trappers there an amazing story.

Colter said he had seen springs of boiling water and rocks that spouted steam and water hundreds of feet in the air. The trappers shook their heads sadly. They decided that Colter's trouble with the Blackfeet had caused him to lose his mind. Later, however, other mountain men found the land that had been called "Colter's Hell." These unique formations are what we now call hot spring geysers.

While the trappers talked about adventure, Ashley and Henry were discussing their business problems.

"We are not in very good shape right now," said Ashley. "We've lost a lot of goods and horses and we have only twenty-five packs of fur."

"True," agreed Henry, "and we run the risk of losing more goods if we try to go on up the Missouri past the Ree villages. We will have to go overland to the Yellowstone, and that will be a hard trip because we are short of packhorses."

Ashley thought a moment. Then he said, "I think it is time we considered changing our way of operating."

"How do you mean?"

"I mean," said Ashley, "that we should not try to hold a fort near the Yellowstone and at other points east of the Rocky Mountains. Instead, we should send out small parties of trappers west of the mountains."

"An excellent idea!" Henry exclaimed. "West of the Rockies our trappers won't run into so many Blackfeet or trappers hired by other fur companies." He was silent a moment, thinking it over, then asked, "How would we collect the furs that our men get, Ashley?"

"That's no problem. Each summer we will have all of our trappers meet at a central rendezvous. We can send word out during the winter and spring telling where this meeting place will be. We can change it if necessary to stay near the trapping grounds.

"At the rendezvous, our trappers can turn in their furs and get supplies for another trapping season. A lot of trappers who are on their own will also come to the rendezvous to trade their furs for powder, bullets, and other goods. I have discussed this plan with Jim Clyman and we both think it will work."

"I think so too, General. It is a good plan," said Henry. "The chance to exchange tall tales as well as furs will bring trappers from all over the West to our rendezvous!"

"My first step," said Ashley, "will be to go to St. Louis and borrow enough money to buy supplies for sale at the rendezvous. Meanwhile, we should divide our present party of trappers and send them into the fur country."

"I suggest that we send out two parties," said Henry. "I will send Jed Smith, Jim Clyman, and a dozen more men to Powder River country. The rest of the men I will take to the Yellowstone. We'll rejoin the twenty trappers I left at the fort. Then from there I will send trapping parties up the Yellowstone and over into the Big Horn River country."

"Where will most of the trappers spend the winter?" asked Ashley.

"Several parties probably will camp with the Crows in Wind River country," replied Henry. "The Crows hate the Blackfeet, and in case of trouble we can count on them for some help. Then in the spring our trapping parties can move into the country west of the Rocky Mountains."

"Excellent," said Ashley. "Keep in touch with me by messenger so I can arrange to bring supplies to our first rendezvous."

CHAPTER 10
Jed Whips a Grizzly

At the head of a small band of trappers, Jed Smith rode along a wooded slope east of the Powder River. With Jed were Jim Clyman, Art Black, William Sublette, Dave Jackson, and Hank Johnson, the man whose jaw Jed had broken in St. Louis.

Jed had left the Cheyenne several weeks earlier with the party that Major Henry had ordered to go to Powder River country. Then Jed had convinced Tom Fitzpatrick that it would be a good idea to split the party into two bands. Tom would take command of one band and Jed the other.

"Large trapping parties scare the beaver out of the country. Even fifteen men make a lot of noise," Jed had argued. "A small band gets better results."

"It does," Fitzpatrick had agreed, "if it doesn't run into Blackfeet. A large band of trappers may get fewer pelts but the trappers have a better chance of keeping their scalps. I hope a Blackfoot doesn't get yours," Fitzpatrick had said.

"God willing, no Blackfoot is going to get my scalp," Jed had answered as he swung into the saddle and waved good-bye to Fitzpatrick. He had no way of knowing that he soon would nearly lose his scalp to an enemy much more fierce than a Blackfoot warrior.

Two days after leaving Fitzpatrick, Jed's men reached the slope east of the Powder River. As Jed was riding around a clump of bushes, his horse gave a frightened snort and lunged to one side.

Jed was pulling hard on the bridle when a huge grizzly bear smashed into the horse and knocked Jed from the saddle. As he hit the ground, Jed grabbed his knife. The grizzly lunged across the horse's body and swung a heavy paw tipped with sharp claws. Jed felt a cutting pain in his side. He ducked and plunged his knife into the grizzly.

Then Jed suddenly found himself looking squarely into the grizzly's dripping mouth. He twisted away but the animal's jaws struck the top of Jed's head.

Blinded by blood, Jed still kept swinging his knife at the grizzly. Then he hurled himself to one side with all the strength he could collect to escape the grizzly's next lunge. Jed was on his knees, swinging his knife and wiping blood from his eyes when he heard Art Black speaking.

"Take it easy, Jed," Art was saying. "The grizzly's had enough of the argument. In fact, too much. He's dead."

Jed was aware of men lifting and carrying him. He was dizzy with pain. His head was on fire, and his side hurt savagely.

"What do you know?" Hank Johnson exclaimed. "That grizzly ripped Jed's scalp off as slick as if a Blackfoot'd done it! Almost took his ear off, too!"

"Get some water so we can wash him off and see what's left," said Art Black.

Jed took a deep breath and sat up. "Jim," he said weakly, "get a needle and thread from my pack. You've got some sewing to do."

"How about a drink, Jed?" asked Hank Johnson. He stopped and rubbed his jaw, remembering that night in St. Louis. Then added, "This sure is a time when a man could use a drink."

"Thanks, Hank," Jed replied. "I won't need one. Jim is mighty gentle with a needle."

Hank Johnson pulled at his beard. "Jed may be kinda soft talking like a preacher with his hymns and all," he said to one man in particular. "But when I sees that grizzly, I says there ain't another man like Jed in these parts!"

Jim Clyman carefully sewed up the cut running from Jed's left eyebrow across his forehead. Then he sewed Jed's scalp and left ear back in place. He took off what remained of Jed's hunting shirt and tested his ribs. He found four broken ribs and put a strip of buckskin around Jed's body.

"Want us to carry you back to camp, Jed?" Jim asked.

"No, I'll ride if you have a horse handy," replied Jed.

"Ride my horse," Art Black said. Then, grinning, he added, "Of course, any man who's tough enough to whip a grizzly ought to be able to walk to camp."

"Thank you, Art," said Jed. "I think I'll ride. I don't feel very tough right now."

Back at camp, Jim treated Jed's wounds with a dressing of soap and sugar. That night for once Jed didn't join the trappers. He lay in his tent and read his Bible while the men talked for hours about his fight with the grizzly.

Jed amazed even the tough mountain men by getting back to his trapping in about ten days. But for many months, his torn eyebrow and head made him a fearful sight. "You better not look into a clear pool of water," the men would say to him. "What you see might scare you to death."

"Well," Jed would answer, "maybe I can scare the Blackfeet into leaving us alone while we trap."

They were moving gradually westward. One day, the trappers met a band of Crow Indians. The handsome warriors, dressed in their buckskin, were so friendly that the trappers wanted to rest in their camp.

Jed saw that the Crows were much cleaner than most Indians he had seen in the Missouri country. He made plans to come back to their winter camp on the Wind River. It would be as good a place as they could find to spend the winter months.

After a few days with the Crows, Jed's men went back to trapping beaver. They kept busy on the Powder River and neighboring streams in what would one day be Montana and Wyoming. But as soon as the fall trapping ended, Jed's band headed southwestward. They were bound for the Crow winter camp.

Food was scarce along the way, and they hurried to get to the camp.

"If we don't hit it pretty soon," said Art Black, "I am going to have to eat my extra pair of moccasins and my shirt fringes."

"Well, I've done that a few times in the years I have been traveling over this country," Jim Clyman said.

"What's that yelling up ahead?" Art Black suddenly asked.

"That ain't yellin'," said Jim. "That is Jed singin' a Methodist hymn. He says it makes him feel better to sing hymns when things are a little tough."

"I'll be dogged if that Jed Smith doesn't do something to surprise me just about every day!" exclaimed Art. "His way of life and how he lives out his faith is mighty tempting to an aimless mountain man."

"I admit, Jed is a curious feller," Jim agreed. "But there ain't a better mountain man around. Ain't likely ever to be a better one come along."

"That is a natural fact," said Art. "Every time I think of how I worried about Jed the night I first met him in St. Louis, I have to laugh. I didn't think he'd get along out here in the wilderness. How wrong I was!"

Hungry and numb with cold, the trappers finally reached the Crow camp. The Crows greeted them noisily. The Indians—men, women, and children were all excited about the buffalo hunt, which was to take place the next day. The white men had come, the warriors said, just in time to help them bring in the winter's meat.

Early the next morning the whole camp was astir. There was running here and running there, and the air was filled with excitement.

Horses neighed, dogs barked. No one talked about anything except buffalo, horses, rifles, arrows, knives. To the surprise of the trappers, the hunters had laid aside their buckskins.

Although it was freezing cold, the Crows had come out stripped to the waist. They would be hot enough, they said, before the hunt was over.

But now everything was ready. Everybody was heading for the valley where the hunt would take place.

The hunters, mounted on their horses, and the trappers, mounted on theirs, rode ahead. Behind, trailed the old men, the squaws, and the children. For everybody had a job to do when the big hunt was on. Everybody had to help bring in the meat and the hides.

As soon as they reached the valley, some of the hunters and all the trappers took up positions on either side. There they sat on their horses and waited.

The hunters who had the best horses had, meantime, swung in behind the buffalo herd. With a burst of whooping and yelling, they rode at the animals, driving them to where the main body of hunters waited with guns and bows.

Rifles cracked, arrows whizzed. Buffalo after buffalo fell. A thousand would fall in that day's hunting and the next. Behind the hunters, the old men, the women, and the children worked to strip off the hides and cut up the meat.

There were high spirits in the camp that night. The winter could come now if it would. There would be food enough for all— no one would go hungry when the snow lay heavy on the ground.

The snows came before long, and the winds with them. The trappers learned that the Wind River had not received its name for nothing. Icy blasts howled around the camp. When the snow fell, the wind drifted it high around the skin lodges where the trappers lived.

But inside the lodges it was snug. Jed could forget about wind and snow as he sat stripping bark from cottonwood branches to feed to his horses. In his pot, a buffalo hump would be cooking. By the fire his moccasins would be warming. On his willow frame bed lay a whole pile of buffalo robes. Heavy skins hung over the door. Curtains kept out the wind.

It was easy to stay snug in your lodge and let the wind howl and the snow drift. But Jed was restless. He wanted to explore more of the white areas on the map of North America.

He would pick up a map of the region beyond the Rocky Mountains—Shining Mountains, the Indians called them. This map had too many white spaces on it to suit Jed. He had heard the Crows talk of a pass through the Rocky Mountains. He wanted to find it.

Late in February, fifteen trappers with Jed at their head rode out of the Crow camp. The Crows said that if you went up the Sweetwater River you would find a pass through the mountains. Jed was making for that river. It was still bitterly cold weather, but Jed had waited as long as he could. He felt the Lord was driving him forward to find out what lay beyond the Rockies.

In the Sweetwater valley, Jed and Jim decided to have the men make a cache. They had brought their whole store of furs on packhorses, and they didn't want to be bothered with furs now. It would be best to hide everything they didn't want to take beyond the mountains.

"First thing to do when you make a cache," said Jim, "is to send out guards to see that no Indians are around. No use to hide somethin' in the ground if Indians are near."

They had to satisfy him. Not until Jim was sure there were no Indians anywhere near would he start on the cache. But then he fell to work with a will. He had the men dig a large hole in the ground. Every shovelful of earth had to be laid carefully on buffalo robes.

Then Jim told the men to tunnel back under the ground for several yards. He showed the trappers how to line the tunnel with brush and grass. Then Jim and Jed and Art packed the tunnel with furs and all the goods they didn't need. The hole leading down to the tunnel they filled with earth. The left-over soil the trappers carried to the river.

When that was done, Jim said the cache was finished except for the final touches. All signs of the digging must be wiped out. Horses must be penned over the cache so their hooves would destroy the signs. Afterwards, ashes from their campfire must be scattered over the cache.

Art Black wiped the sweat from his face and laughed. "No one should be able to find this cache," he said. "Think we will be able to remember where it is?"

"Jim's like a dog that buries a bone," said Jed. "He always knows where to go back and dig for it."

Westward, ever westward moved Jed and his men. They followed the Sweetwater River into a broad valley that led gradually up into the mountains. It was there that their troubles began. Once again the trappers ran short of food. For fifteen days they had no water save that from melted snow. But Jed pushed on, and his men followed him grimly.

Then one day the weary band reached the Continental Divide. That was a great moment for them. They had always heard that all water on the east side of this high point flowed into the Gulf of Mexico and the Atlantic Ocean. All water on the west side flowed into the Gulf of California and the Pacific Ocean.

It seemed wonderful to stand on the roof of America. Jed threw sticks into neighboring streams. One stick floated toward the east and the other floated toward the west.

"That east-bound stick," said Art Black thoughtfully, "will finally reach the Mississippi River and go on down to the Gulf of Mexico. But where do you think the west-bound stick will go before it finally reaches the Pacific Ocean?"

"No one knows yet," answered Jed. "The map shows a river called the Buenaventura. It is supposed to flow from the Rockies to the Pacific. Someday I am going out there and really see if there is such a river."

On the western side of the Continental Divide, Jed and his men found a country full of beaver. Indians had told them the beavers there were almost waiting around to be caught in traps, and that's about the way it was.

But somehow the trapping didn't interest Jed as it once had done. He had started to fill in the white spaces on the maps, and beavers weren't exciting any more. He wanted to go on exploring and charting paths in the wilderness areas that could be helpful to others.

He and his men had traveled through the famous South Pass of the Rocky Mountains. They had found a trail that thousands of pioneers would use when they went to California and Oregon in the 1840s and 1850s. But to Jed it seemed he had done very little as yet. The prospect of future usefulness and of adventure lured him on. What were hunger and thirst and weariness when you could have the thrill of standing where no trailblazer had ever stood before?

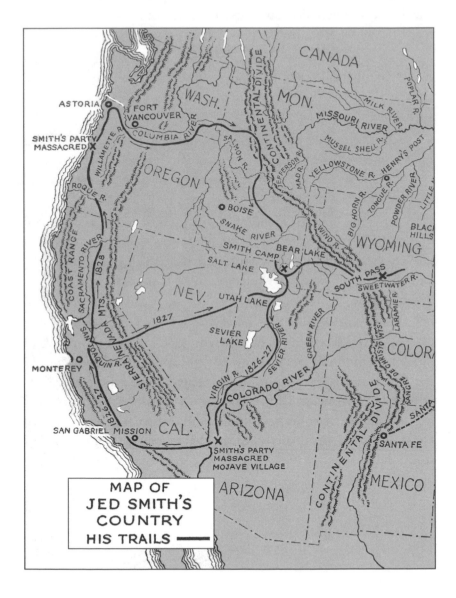

MAP OF
JED SMITH'S
COUNTRY
HIS TRAILS ━━━

CHAPTER 11

Jed Starts on His Big Adventure

A busy year of trapping had passed, and now it was time for the big rendezvous. Trappers from north, south, east, and west came to the banks of Henry's Fork on the Green River in the summer of 1825. Many of these men asked, "Where is Jed Smith? What's he up to?"

Jed was busy far to the north and west. Several months before the date of the rendezvous, Andrew Henry had decided to retire, and Jed had been given command of all Ashley trappers. Major Henry had had enough of Indian raids. Too many of his men had been killed and too many horses stolen.

Jed had taken his men to Snake River country and north to the Columbia River. While trapping, he took the time to explore what would one day be the Canadian border. On his way back, he rode past the Great Salt Lake. Few trailblazers had done that as yet.

When he arrived at the rendezvous, more than six hundred trappers and Indians were camped there. It was like a state fair, only a lot wilder. Ashley had brought a large supply of trade goods and soon was doing a big business. Sugar, coffee, tobacco, powder, bullets, rifles, blankets, kettles, beads, and all sorts of trinkets were exchanged for piles of fur and buffalo robes.

Snake and Ute Indians, Canadians, Virginians, New Englanders, Kentuckians, Westerners, and Europeans gathered around fires at night to drink and sing.

During the day, they held all sorts of contests. They ran, jumped, shot guns and arrows, and raced horses. Ponies, blankets, knives, and kettles were won and lost in noisy games. At night, trappers and Indians would join in a wild dance around the fire.

"Guess most of them figure they won't be alive next year," said Jim Clyman as he and Jed stood by to watch the dancing, "so they're lettin' off some steam while they can."

When the rendezvous ended, Ashley had a huge pile of furs to take back to St. Louis. Jim Clyman and fifty men were to go along with the general and his valuable load down the Missouri to St. Louis.

Shortly before he left, Jim took Jed by the arm and led him aside. "Well," he said, "guess I won't be seein' you for quite a spell."

"Why, Jim, you should be back in a month or so," Jed said, surprised.

"No. I'm through with trappin' Jed. I aim to get myself a piece of land in Missouri and settle down. I'm getting too old and stiff for this sort of life. Think I'll quit before my hair is hangin' in some Blackfoot's lodge."

"There is no Blackfoot alive that can get you, Jim," said Jed. "And you're not old."

"I'm old enough to know that I better quit," said Jim.

Jed swallowed hard. Jim had been his teacher, companion, and friend. He seemed closer in many ways than the members of Jed's own family. Jed's eyes grew misty at the thought of parting, after he and Jim had shared so much adventure, danger, and hardship.

"Jim," Jed finally said, "I don't know what to say to you except that I thank the Almighty for your kindness. I owe you so much, and things won't be the same out here with you gone. It is my prayer that you will find peace with God and man on your land in Missouri."

"Who knows, friend," responded Jim, "maybe I will become a praying man like yourself some day. Lord knows I could use some peace in this here heart."

They shook hands. Neither man said another word as they walked toward Jim's horse. Jim climbed silently into the saddle. The man who had always had so much to say about everything didn't want to say anything now. He waved his hand and rode away.

During the next year, Jed thought often of Jim. In his loneliness, he found that Art Black was a good man to have around. Art could joke when he was knee-deep in an icy beaver stream or riding through the wilderness without a thing to eat for several days.

But that was a long year for Jed, his first without Jim, and he was glad when another summer and another rendezvous rolled round. This time it was being held in a different place, at Bear Lake near the border of what would be the states of Utah and Idaho. And this time a different sort of surprise was waiting for him.

One day toward the end of the rendezvous, Ashley called Jed to his tent. William Sublette and Dave Jackson were there, too.

"Jed," said Ashley, "I have decided to sell out, and I've chosen you three men to sell out to. I will continue to supply you with trading goods, but you men will own the business. Sublette and Jackson are willing. What do you say?"

"Why, I'm glad of the chance, General," said Jed. "I will look forward to working with partners like Bill and Dave."

They shook hands all around. Then Sublette said, "We've got some planning to do right away. It is our idea that I should be our businessman. I'll handle the buying and selling. Dave will direct the trapping parties. And you will be in charge of finding new beaver trapping country."

"Suits me fine," replied Jed. "I've been thinking a little in the past year of striking out for the Southwest."

"That's no secret to us," laughed Dave Jackson. "We've seen that look in your eyes. And we know what going southwest means. It means that you and your men are going to do a lot of traveling and very little eating during the next year. But if that's where you want to go, we are willing."

Jed hurried back to his tent to study his maps again. Beyond the Great Salt Lake was an unknown country. Maybe it contained streams full of beaver. Maybe the great and mysterious Buenaventura

River flowed through that country. If it did, what a find that would be for trappers!

They would no longer have to use the difficult and dangerous route down the Missouri to St. Louis. They could float their furs down the Buenaventura to the Pacific Ocean.

A few days later, Jed was busy getting ready for his great adventure. William Sublette and Art Black watched him as he went over a list of supplies.

"You will be going into an unknown country, Jed," said Sublette. "Your chances of coming back are not very good."

"If what I do is right, the good Lord will give me the strength to do it and the mercy to survive it," said Jed.

"Men have been in the right before and still failed to do something they wanted to do," Art Black pointed out.

"If I fail," Jed replied, "it will be because the Lord has a grander purpose in view than my personal happiness—and that is fine with me. Besides which, the only way that I can truly fail is if I fear to attempt what I believe to be God's will for my life."

When Jed had gone off to look over piles of supplies, Sublette said, "He puzzles me with his religious talk. Just the same, I wish I was going along with Jed. His strength seems to flow into you. It makes you stronger just to look at him."

Art Black nodded. "I've been following Jed for several years," he said, "and I'm going to follow him till I drop. I want to go along and see what's over the next range of mountains, and I know that Jed will take me there and bring me back! He is a man of his word."

"How do the other men feel about this trip?" asked Sublette.

"Jed called for volunteers. Twenty men answered," Art Black continued. "I think he will take most of them, and I'll bet most of them will stick by Jed. He can get men to believe in him in a mighty short time!"

Not long afterwards, Jed Smith led seventeen men out of the rendezvous. They traveled single file, each leading one or more packhorses or mules. The pack animals were loaded with beaver traps, powder, food, and all sorts of goods for Indians. On one horse Jed had hung chests containing his records, his Bible, his Methodist hymnbook, and several books of history.

CHAPTER 12

Jed Rides into the Unknown

The route Jed had chosen took them past the Great Salt Lake down into country that was anything but pleasant. Sandy wastes and bare hills stretched out as far as the eye could see.

The men had come to trap beaver. They began to grumble, saying they could see no reason for Jed's taking them to a place like this. But Jed did not stop. Day after day, he grimly kept the men moving.

The blazing sun beat down upon them. The rivers they came to were nearly dry. There was almost no grass for the animals. Now and again, horses and mules began to drop from lack of water and grass. Lack of game forced the men to eat the pitiful animals that had died.

The spirits of the men were low. Gloomily, they rode through the deep and dark passes. Once in a while, the men moved to higher points from which they could see strange towers of stone glistening in the sun. But only Art Black had the spirit to think them wonderful.

"Amazing country!" he would say. "Look at those colors on the rocks!"

"Amazin'!" others would snap back. "Amazin' enough to kill a man!"

"Just pointing out some of the sights so you ladies would enjoy the trip," Art would answer cheerfully.

At night, many of the men sat silent by the fires. They would notice Jed sitting apart, reading his Bible or writing in his record journal, and they would wonder, "What is he after?"

"Jed's playing with death," someone would grumble. "What is out there that we have to see?"

"We won't know till we get there," Art Black would answer. "And I for one don't want to miss it."

As Jed moved south, more horses and mules died each day. The expedition had started out with fifty animals. By the time it reached the Colorado River, only twenty-eight horses and mules were left. And these were much too heavily loaded. They carried not only their own packs but also those of the animals that had died. Rich grass had to be found soon; else all the animals would be lost.

Several men began to urge Jed to turn back.

"It would be more dangerous to turn back now than to go ahead," Jed replied. "We must have food for ourselves and grass for our horses. But we will get them quicker if we keep moving south. I promise you that we will reach an Indian village or Spanish settlement in two days, or three at the most."

Two days later, on the west side of the Colorado River, the exhausted men came upon an Indian village lying in a rich valley.

"How in thunder did Jed know we'd find this place in two

days?" the amazed men asked one another.

"I don't know whether he really did know it," replied Art. "But Jed does have a sure faith in his work and the Lord. Also, Jed's got a feeling for the land, no matter where he goes. When he searches the country with those sharp eyes of his, I get a feeling that he can see through mountains."

"I don't follow all your fancy talk," said one man who had done a lot of grumbling. "But I know now that Jed is a leader I want to follow!"

The trappers looked curiously at the four-sided log huts no more than three feet high and at the Indians slowly coming forward waving their bows. Jed had gone ahead to meet them. To put the Indians at ease, he was giving the sign of peace.

Seeing this, the Indians put down their bows and came closer. They were Mojaves, they made Jed understand. Their hearts were good. They would trade. They would give the weary men food.

For fifteen days the half-starved trappers feasted on Mojave fish, beans, corn, pumpkins, and wheat. But though the Mojaves were so friendly to them, Jed warned his men to be always on their guard.

"The Mojaves probably will cause no trouble if we are watchful and treat them right. Make sure that you do treat them right. With my own hands, I will whip the first trapper who causes any trouble while we are here."

By the time Jed was ready to go on, his horses and mules were in good condition. They had had their fill of grass. Jed traded goods for a few more horses and then had his supplies taken across the river. With two Indian guides to lead the way, he headed directly west into the Mojave Desert.

The Indians had told Jed that he was going into dangerous country, and the trappers were not long in finding that out. The Mojave Desert was much worse than the terrible land they had traveled through on their way to the Colorado.

For one whole day, the men stumbled over glistening white salt. In the daytime, the heat was almost more than they could bear. It was so hot that finally Jed hit upon the idea of having the men dig holes in the sand where they might rest. This helped, and the trappers pushed on through a land where almost nothing grew except cactus.

Finally, when the exhausted men were barely dragging themselves along, the Indian guides pointed southward to a gap in the snow-covered San Bernardino Mountains. "Come on, men!" Jed shouted joyfully. "There will be food and water and rest when we get through that gap ahead of us."

Jed's words gave the men new courage. They stumbled on, leading the few horses and mules that were still alive. But worse awaited them at the gap. When they reached the mountains, the steep trail punished the exhausted men and pack animals. Jed kept moving up and down the trail to urge the men on and to help fallen men to their feet.

"I don't know how you do it," one of these said. "But if you can keep going, I guess I can." With this he gave a mighty pull at the lead rope and dragged his heavily loaded mule a few steps up the trail.

Jed fell to his knees when he reached the top and looked down into the green valley beyond. His heart was very full. He thanked God for helping him bring his men through desert and mountain.

Art stumbled down beside him. "I've followed you over another range of mountains," he said, "and I like what I see."

Fresh, sparkling water, such as they had dreamed about in the desert, rolled through the rich green valley. Cattle and horses in huge herds peacefully fed in that green. Beyond, to the west and

southeast, snow-capped peaks of mountains towered. To the south, lower mountains stretched.

Art could not take his eyes from the stream and the grass, the horses and the cattle. But Jed was dreamily gazing off to the west. "I didn't find the Buenaventura River," he was thinking. "There probably isn't any such river from the east to the west. But I have filled in a big white space on the map."

The ragged, half-starved trappers wasted no time getting down the trail. They had only one thought in mind—water.

"This is the wettest water I ever tasted," Art Black remarked when he had at last drunk his fill.

"All water is wet," one of the other trappers answered. Then, smiling at Art he added, "Maybe you're right, though. It sure tastes wetter than any we've had for a long, long time!"

Later that day, while the men lay idly talking or dozing, some Mexican soldiers rode up. Their officer took one look at the hungry men and ordered a cow to be killed and roasted. For the trappers it was a feast. They couldn't seem to get enough, and their spirits rose with every bite.

When, a few days later, Jed ordered his men to move on, they acted as though they had forgotten all about the terrible Mojave Desert.

CHAPTER 13

Jed Conquers Mountain and Desert

On November 27, 1826, the trappers arrived at the Franciscan mission of San Gabriel. Two men from the mission at once visited Jed and invited him to spend the night with the brothers. Jed gratefully accepted. The trappers had plenty of meat and cornbread that night, and in the morning wandered about admiring the beautiful scenery.

The mission of San Gabriel seemed to be very rich. The Franciscan brothers had thousands of horses, cattle, and sheep in the fields. The friars told them that the grazing lands of the mission ran all the way to the sea.

Jed learned from Father Sanchez that around 2,500 Indians lived near the mission church or in the villages out on the grazing lands. Father Sanchez and the other friars directed the work in the orchards, vineyards, soap works, and in the weaving and sewing rooms.

"While you are here," Father Sanchez said, while showing Jed around, "we must talk much about your country. Here at San Gabriel we feel far away from things and are anxious to get news from the East. Of course, you will have to go soon to San Diego and see the Provincial Governor, Jose Maria Echeandia."

Father Sanchez frowned a little and then added, "I trust that the governor will welcome you, but one never knows about those things."

Jed was a little taken back by this. He thought a moment, and then he said slowly, "My men have no papers permitting them to travel in California. They do not have trapping licenses. I guess the governor has the law on his side if he wants to arrest us."

Father Sanchez put his hand on Jed's shoulder. "Go, my son," he said, "and speak truthfully to the governor. I feel that he will not be unkind even though you have no licenses. Leave your men here and go alone."

The news that Jed and his men were in California was not long in reaching Governor Echeandia. For several days before Jed arrived in San Diego, the governor had been worrying about him.

"It is all right that Americans come to California in ships," he said to his secretary. "But now they slip through the mountains behind our backs. That is quite another thing. That is serious. But what can I do?"

"You could arrest them and then put them on an American ship in the harbor?" suggested the secretary.

"Yes, I could. But then what happens? My government already is having trouble with the American officers in Washington. This Smith may be important, you can never tell about these wild Americans. Then the government in Washington becomes angry and my government will probably blame everything on me! What can I do then?"

As the secretary had no answer, the governor continued. "But now, suppose, I am oh, so nice to this Smith. What happens then? My enemies will no doubt report me to the government. They will say I am letting dangerous spies run loose in this province. Oh!

Why do these things happen to me?" The governor glared at his secretary, who still had no answer.

By the time Jed arrived, the Governor had not made up his mind how to act. He began by asking questions.

"Why did you come to California? What could be out here that interests you Americans?"

Jed explained that he had lost most of his horses in the Mojave Desert and was forced to push on through the mountains or die.

"But you cannot stay here," replied Echeandia. "You should be in jail. You have no papers, no permits. You have no business in this province."

"I have no wish to stay here and cause you trouble," replied Jed. "May I have permission to move north to Oregon and cross the mountains back to my own country?"

"I do not think that is possible," said Echeandia.

He studied the tall, clean-shaven man with the scarred eyebrow and the sharp eyes. It had been reported that Jed had seventeen heavily armed men at San Gabriel. An attempt to arrest them might bring on a bloody fight. That would get the governor into trouble with officers in Mexico.

But he couldn't let these Americans go north through the thinly settled province. This sharp-eyed American would see too much. Then, in a year or two, more Americans would come through the mountains into California.

"What then, is your answer, Governor?" Jed asked. "I wish only to leave your country peacefully. But I do not want to risk the lives of my men by crossing the Mojave Desert again."

"Return in two days and I shall give you my answer," replied the governor. An idea had struck him while Jed was speaking.

As soon as he was alone, the governor rang for his secretary. "I understand there are six American merchants in San Diego," Echeandia said. "Tell those gentlemen I would like to see them as soon as possible."

Jed was ready to accept any plan so long as he did not have to face the desert again. He hoped the governor would change his mind, but he was not at all sure what the answer would be.

"I have here," the governor began, "a paper signed by six of your countrymen. They live in our San Diego. These gentlemen have satisfied me that your intentions are peaceful. I cannot, however, allow you to go north to Oregon. You must return by the route you followed when you came here. But I will help you get supplies."

Jed's face had fallen as he listened. He opened his mouth to speak, but the governor stopped him. "Do not argue with me, my friend," Echeandia said, raising his hand. "I have done all I can do."

Jed turned and walked rapidly from the room while the governor, smiling happily, tapped the paper he held. If the government objected to his treatment of Smith, he could show them this paper signed by six important Americans. Everybody would see that he was a wise officer, a good man to rule the Province of California.

Back in San Gabriel, Jed quickly collected horses and supplies for his journey. He had no intention of obeying the governor's orders. "There is a lot of wilderness in this province," Jed said to himself, "and the governor cannot control us when we move away from the coast. I will not knowingly risk the lives of my men on account of his order. God has called me, in the sixth commandment, to preserve life whenever possible, and I mean to obey my Maker's orders."

In February the trappers crossed the San Bernardino Mountains through a pass, skirted the Mojave Desert, and climbed the Tehachapi Mountains. Jed expected to find wilderness beyond, and he was not disappointed. The San Joaquin Valley was a huge wilderness filled with wild animals—deer, wild horses, antelope, beaver, and bears.

No one bothered the trappers, and they moved rapidly north till they reached a branch of the San Joaquin River. Here Jed decided to build a camp. It was his plan to leave most of his men in California while he tried to find another way back toward the east.

In May, Jed, Art Black and Silas Gobel, with seven horses and two mules, left the camp. In the Sierra Nevada Mountains the snow was still more than seven feet deep. The howling winds battered them as they moved along narrow trails, looking for a pass.

Who could guess where it might be? They would start up one trail only to find that towering cliffs shut them in on three sides. Then all they could do was retrace their steps and try another trail. Three times in a single day they thought they were on the right trail, and three times they had to retrace their steps.

But finally one day, they took a trail that led them up and up to the very top of the Sierras and down on the other side. They had found the pass at last! Two horses and a mule had been lost doing it, but Jed, Art, and Silas thought it a small price to pay.

They had crossed the Sierras—something no other non-Indian men had ever done.

Now the sun-baked Nevada plains were before them. To Jed and Art and Silas they were a welcome change at first. But before long the men found themselves wishing for the snow again. Their eyes ached from the heat, their throats burned with thirst. They were exhausted even before they reached the Great Salt Desert.

But now it was pain, pain every step of the way. The winds swept stinging salt in their faces. The shifting sand dragged at their feet. The salt-covered ground became as hot as the top of a stove. Four of their five horses died as they dragged themselves across this deadly land.

Through all this, Art Black had done no complaining. But now an hour came when he fell to his knees and then crawled to a juniper tree. "I've followed you as far as I can go, Jed," he panted. "This time I won't live to find out where we're going."

Jed took Silas by the arm. "Come on, Silas," he said. "We've got to push on and find water!"

But Silas dropped down, too. Jed pulled him to his feet. "We can't quit now, Silas," Jed cried. "I'm sure there is a mountain only a few miles ahead! There will be water at the mountain!"

"There ain't no mountain out there," Silas answered hopelessly. "You think you see a mountain, but it's just one of them mirages that have been driving us crazy for days." And again Silas fell. Again Jed dragged him to his feet. Together they stumbled on.

Afterwards Jed could not say how long they went on this way. All he knew was that suddenly right ahead of them there was a flowing spring.

"No," he thought, "it must be a mirage."

He dragged himself along another few yards, and then half closed his eyes and looked again. The spring was still there. "Silas!" he cried. "Water! A spring!"

Silas Gobel raised his head, looked wildly about, and for an instant fixed his eyes crazily on the flowing spring. Then he hurled himself toward the water. He lay in the shallow pool and drank and drank. Jed wanted to throw himself in the pool, too, and drink and drink. But he only knelt down and took up some water in his hand and drank a little. Silas was still swallowing great mouthfuls.

"You'll kill yourself," Jed cried, dragging him away.

Jed got out a kettle and brought water to Silas where he lay, then returned to the spring and took another drink. Afterwards he filled a kettle and started back to find Art.

Art was stretched out flat on his stomach under the juniper. He was breathing heavily through his open mouth. Jed rolled him over and tipped the kettle. Art choked a little, then opened his eyes and grabbed the kettle from Jed.

He had swallowed a good half before Jed could get the water away from him.

Art lay back on the ground moaning, "Man could die for want

of a drink, and you bring him a spoonful!"

"You've had too much now, Art! If you have any more, right now, it will make you sick! Come on and get up! We've got to get to Silas before he kills himself drinking!"

Six days later, Art, Jed, and Silas approached the Bear Lake rendezvous. They were in a pitiful state—ragged, hungry, exhausted. All that was left out of the nine animals they had started out with from California was one horse and one mule. These were so weak that they could hardly carry the few articles loaded on them.

A lookout at Bear Lake had spotted the three men while they were still at a distance and had fired his rifle in the air. Now as Jed, Art, and Silas came in, dozens of trappers ran shouting and cheering to receive them. A cannon was fired off, for Jed and his men had been given up for lost.

The trappers looked in amazement at the scarecrows from out of the desert. It was hard to believe that these three had really crossed the Great Salt Lake Desert. They had done what no one had ever done before, something that would be remembered as often as men talked about the winning of the West.

CHAPTER 14
Back to California

Before long, Jed was busy planning another trip to California. It was true that he already had done a lot to fill in the white spaces on the maps. He had crossed the Mojave Desert and reached California. He had found a pass through the towering Sierra Nevada Mountains. And he had crossed the burning Great Salt Lake Desert. He also had proved that the Buenaventura River did not flow west through the mountains to the Pacific Ocean.

There was more to do, however. He was determined to find this mysterious Buenaventura River. More important, he had to go back and get the men he had left on the Stanislaus River in California. These men were depending on Jed Smith to keep his word.

Silas Gobel shook his head in amazement as he watched Jed get ready for another trip. "Three days ago," exclaimed Silas, "Old Jed was about half dead after crossing the Salt Lake Desert. Now, he acts like he'd been sittin' under a tree all spring. How in thunder does he do it?"

"Jed just doesn't seem to be like other men," replied Art Black. Then he smiled and asked Silas a question. "Are you going back to California with him? I am. This man and his God are both worth following."

"Of course," said Silas. "Men that follow Old Jed don't get much rest, but I'm not quittin' now."

"Why do you call him 'Old Jed'?" asked Art. "He's only 28 years old and you are past 50."

Silas scratched his head and then replied, "Seems natural. Since

Old Jed took us across the Salt Lake Desert, he seems older and wiser than any of us will ever be."

Ten days after he arrived at the rendezvous, Jed started out again with eighteen men. They headed south for the Colorado River and the Mojave villages. Jed was following almost the same route he had used the year before, so they made good time. Knowing the way, Jed could take short cuts, which saved them a lot of time.

"How in thunder can Old Jed remember this trail so well?" Silas Gobel wondered. "I believe he recognizes every rock, tree, and bush he saw when we came through here last year!"

"I don't know how he does it, but I'm sure glad he does," Art an–swered. "I'm sure he would tell you that it is part of how the Creator gives talent to men so's they can get done with the work He gives 'em."

It seemed only a short time before they were back in the Mojave village where the Indians had been so friendly to them a year ago. The Mojaves seemed to be just as friendly now. Corn, beans, and fish were set before the grateful men.

The Indians traded as before. They seemed just as pleased with the presents Jed made them. But though Jed and his men did not know it, secretly the Indians were getting their bows and arrows and war clubs ready.

Something had happened between Jed's two visits that had angered the Indians. Jed never found out what it was. All he knew was that the Indians, with whom he had seemed to be the best of friends, suddenly turned on him.

Jed was just leaving when it happened. He and five men had already crossed the Colorado. The rest of the party were preparing to drive the horses and mules across the river. All of a sudden Art Black seized Jed by the arm and screamed, "The Mojaves! They're attacking our men!"

Jed swung around to look. What he saw on the other side of the river made his blood run cold.

Showers of arrows were falling on Silas and the men with him. Then, while Jed and his companions looked on helplessly, the Mojaves, with whoops and yells rushed upon the remaining men. Art Black raised his rifle to fire. "Don't!" Jed cried. "We are too far away to hit anyone. We'd better save what powder we have for later on."

The men with Silas didn't have a chance. What could thirteen do against hundreds? The trappers fell beneath the shower of arrows. They were beaten to the ground with war clubs.

Silas Gobel, using his rifle as a club, fought off a dozen Indians. Near him the huge Isaac Galbraith swung his rifle and knocked down three warriors. Two more Mojaves leaped on him, but the six-foot seven-inch giant hurled them to the ground. He looked about him just in time to see Silas Gobel fall with no less than a dozen arrows in his back and chest.

Isaac then saw Tom Virgin stumbling toward the river. Blood was beginning to appear on his head. Isaac ran to him, dragged Tom into the river, and started swimming. Arrows fell all around the two. With one arm around Tom, Isaac swam for the other shore. As he neared it, Jed and Art Black plunged into the river and helped the two men reach the bank.

On the other side of the Colorado, the Mojaves were whooping and dancing wildly. Jed took in the scene and quickly sized things up. He had but seven men left, one of them badly wounded, and only five rifles. All the horses and mules had been lost. A small amount of powder, a few packs of trade goods, and fifteen pounds of dried meat were all he had in the way of supplies.

Jed and his men could not cross the river and return to Bear Lake country. Ahead of them lay one hundred and fifty miles of desert land. Behind them were hundreds of bloodthirsty, howling Mojaves. Jed wasted no time worrying about his troubles.

"Quick," Jed cried. "Scatter these trinkets by the river!" He had ripped open one of the packs of trade goods and was pulling out handfuls of colored buttons, beads, and ribbons. "While the Mojaves are quarreling over these," Jed explained, "we'll get ready to make a stand."

Already he had a plan. Jed ordered the men to run to a small clump of cottonwoods and build a barricade. Working madly, the men cut down branches and piled them high into a sort of wall. They also cut poles and tied butcher knives on them. "These should come in handy if we do any fighting at close quarters," Jed said. "Now get down behind the barricade."

Jed kept his own rifle and gave the rest to Art Black and three other men who were good shots. "Hold your fire," Jed ordered, "until you are dead sure you can hit a Mojave. We can beat them if we keep calm and shoot straight."

"Do you really believe we can beat several hundred Mojaves with five rifles?" asked Art.

"No, I don't," Jed replied. "But keep that to yourself, Art, and don't miss any shots."

Lying side by side, Jed and Art watched the Mojaves creeping towards the barricade. Two of the Indians, bolder than the rest, were getting close.

"They think we can't hit them at this distance," said Jed. "Let's show them. You take the one on the left, and I'll try for the one on the right."

Jed and Art fired at the same instant. Both the Mojaves fell to the ground dead. The other warriors, seeing them fall, let out a howl of fright and ran. They had never used rifles themselves and were still deathly afraid of them.

Jed saw his chance. "Hurry, men!" he cried. "Get the packs collected! We can get away before the Mojaves get up courage enough to attack again!"

One of the trappers helped the wounded Tom Virgin. The others picked up the packs and ran. Behind them the Mojaves were still crouching in fear on the riverbank. They could not seem to make up their minds to face the rifles again.

All night, Jed and his men kept going through the desert. When, early in the morning, they reached a spring, Jed said, "Get your fill of water now, men. We have no way to carry it. We will have to take a chance on finding other springs as we cross."

Through the burning heat of the day, they stayed at the spring; at night they traveled. In the morning they again looked for a spring. Jed found a small pool, and they again spent the day beside it. At night, they went on once more. But at the next spring, they had to stay not only all day but all night, too, because Tom Virgin needed more rest.

The next morning, they pushed on across the burning desert. Hour after hour Jed carried Tom Virgin on his shoulders. The other men became half crazy with thirst, but Jed did not seem to mind the lack of water. "Jed is like those camels you hear about in Africa," Art Black remarked. "They can go for days without drinking."

Jed cut up pieces of cactus with his knife and told the men to chew on them. "You'll get a little juice out of them," he said. "It isn't as good as water, but it will keep you going."

Several times the discouraged men dropped to the ground, but Jed wouldn't let them stay there. "Get up!" he would say. "Keep going! The Lord won't let us die if we keep fighting to live. You can't quit now!"

Finally, Jed and his seven exhausted men reached the Mojave River. It was drier than when Jed had passed it on his first trip across the desert. They followed it for eight miles and came to two Indian lodges.

Jed opened one of his packs and showed the Indians his goods. The red cloth and blue beads caught the Indians' fancy. They were very willing to trade two horses, some cane grass candy, and three stone jars for them. The men filled the jars with water.

On one horse they set Tom Virgin, on the other they loaded their packs. After that they were able to push on more rapidly towards the gap in the mountains, which a year ago the Mojave guides had pointed out.

Once through the gap, Jed and his men felt safe. They were near Mission San Gabriel now and their friend, Father Sanchez. Cattle belonging to the mission were grazing nearby. Cool water and rich green grass were before them. It was a scene of peace and plenty, very welcome to the hungry, thirsty, exhausted men.

Jed let them shoot three of the cows. The men feasted on roast beef, and then dried the rest of the meat to use later on. Jed, of course, took care to send a note to the mission, telling Father Sanchez what he had done and why.

Isaac Galbraith and Tom Virgin carried the message. Tom was to stay at San Gabriel till he recovered from his wound, then go on to San Francisco. As for Isaac, he had had enough of travel and hardship. He made up his mind that he would settle down in California.

At a nearby settlement, Jed traded goods for more horses. Then he got ready to go north and join his men at the camp.

"I don't want to have another argument with Governor Echeandia," Jed said to Art Black. "So I will go on north and let Father Sanchez tell the governor that I'm here again."

When Jed reached his camp, the men were overjoyed to see him. But they no sooner heard about the Indian attack and the death of many of the men they had known, than they lost their good spirits. They thought gloomily about their own chances of getting back to Bear Lake alive.

Jed saw he must not give his men time to sit around and worry. So he quickly told them to get ready to move on north. He and Art Black would, in the meantime, go to the Mission San Jose and get supplies for the trip to northern California and Oregon.

Jed was hoping he could get out of California without having to face Governor Echeandia again. In the providence of God, however, he was unable to avoid him. Father Narcisco Duran of the Mission San Jose had heard of Jed's troubles with Governor Echeandia.

Now that Jed was back again, the Father was sure the American was a spy. "My son," said Father Duran, "my duty is clear. I cannot give you supplies until you see Governor Echeandia. He is in Monterey now. Go to him there."

There was nothing for Jed to do but go. And this time, he knew, the governor would be angrier than ever.

"Why did you fail to let me know you were back in California?" Echeandia demanded when Jed stood before him.

Jed explained to the governor that he thought Father Sanchez would let Echeandia know. Jed said that all he wanted was to get his men out. That was the reason he had come back, and if it hadn't been that the Mojaves attacked him, his party would have been out by now.

"I cannot say that I feel very sorry for you," Echeandia snapped.

The governor was red with anger at this "wild American" who had popped up again just to give him trouble. Echeandia was sick of the problem. He felt like he was right back where he was last year with this wild man Smith. What was to be done?

If he put Jed in jail, the United States government might get angry. Then the Mexican government probably would blame everything on him and he'd lose his job. If, on the other hand, he let Jed roam freely in California, the governor's enemies would stir up trouble.

Echeandia drummed with his fingers on his desk as he considered what to do. Finally he said, "Return in three days and I will tell you what I am going to do with you. But do not expect me to be gentle with a man who acts like a spy!"

Jed started to walk toward the door. "There are several American and British merchants in Monterey," the governor called out after him. "You can tell your story to them. They may believe you. I don't."

The governor was hoping that the American and British merchants would sign some sort of paper promising that Jed would behave himself in California. Then if anything happened, it would be the merchants' fault.

Echeandia was not disappointed. In three days, Jed was back with a paper signed by several British and American merchants. They gave their word that Jed would leave California quickly and peacefully. The governor felt great relief and gave Jed and his men permission to travel north and then east across the mountains to Bear Lake.

CHAPTER 15

Jed Meets the "White-Headed Eagle"

With a good stock of supplies, Jed and his men traveled north and in two weeks reached the banks of a river. Jed was overjoyed when friendly Indians told him that another name for this river, which they called River of the North, was Buenaventura.

That night, Jed got out his map and drew the river in, as he believed it went. No, the Buenaventura did not flow west to the Pacific as mapmakers had drawn it. The river flowed south.

Probably, thought Jed, it went through the Great Valley of California and then on through San Francisco Bay to the Pacific. But in any case there it was. The Buenaventura, which would eventually be called the Sacramento, need no longer be a question mark in his mind.

The going was not easy now. For days, Jed's men struggled through swampy land that made every step hard to take. Pack animals sank in the mud and had to be dragged out by the sweating trappers.

There were plenty of beaver around, but the men were short of traps. A week before, one of Jed's men had deserted and carried off eleven valuable beaver traps. Jed had made no attempt to get the man back. Ever since Jed had ordered him to be whipped for getting drunk and fighting with Indians at the mission, the man had been ugly. Jed was glad to be rid of the deserter—even at a price.

Farther north, the trappers found firmer ground. But here another difficulty arose. The country was swarming with bears. A grizzly seemed to be behind every bush.

"Seems like I'm combing grizzlies out of my hair," Art Black remarked.

"When do you ever comb your hair?" one of the trappers laughed. "You look as hairy as a grizzly yourself."

One day as the men were moving up along a creek, Jed shot a grizzly and was walking toward it when Art shouted, "Look out!" Another grizzly had quietly come out of the bushes a few feet away and was standing there watching Jed. Jed took one look at the open mouth of the grizzly, dropped his rifle, and dove into the creek. Art fired; and when the grizzly fell, he roared with laughter.

"That was a beautiful dive you took!" he shouted to the dripping Jed.

Jed laughed, too, and said, "A grizzly with his mouth open makes me nervous, Art. I got half scalped by one, you'll remember. I'm not anxious to have it done again."

The next day, it was Art who had his troubles with the grizzlies. He had chased a cub into a cave and had foolishly gone in after it. Jed heard loud growls from inside. Then out came Art with the cub's parents roaring mad behind him. The trapper made for a tree and was halfway to the top by the time the grizzlies got to the bottom. They stood there clawing at the trunk, trying to shake him down.

"Art!" yelled Jed. "You're better at climbing than I am at diving. I never saw such speed in all my life."

"I'm sorry I laughed at you, Jed," Art shouted back. "Now will you please do something about these grizzlies! They're shaking the tree so hard I'm having trouble holding on to it!"

"Wait till I stop laughing!" Jed yelled to tease him. "I'm shaking so hard myself I couldn't hit a grizzly even if I wanted to."

The trappers were in good spirits. Grizzlies were all in the day's work, and the men laughed more than they grumbled about them. And they were getting a lot of pelts even though they had so few traps, for the beaver were plentiful. In a single night, the trappers caught twenty, although they had set only twenty-eight traps.

Once the party started north again, Jed spent a lot of time looking for a trail through the Sierra Nevadas. But the towering mountains appeared to be an unbroken wall of rock stretching for miles. At last he gave up. To try to get back to Bear Lake through the Sierras was hopeless, he decided. He would go northwestward toward the coast. "We'll head for Columbia River country, men," Jed said.

It seemed to the trappers that they had been through every kind of country there was, but now again something different was before them. They were in a wild region full of snags, fallen trees, great slippery rocks, and high cliffs. Flooded creeks flowed in all directions through this wilderness.

Jed had to send men ahead to cut a path with axes while the others pulled at the frightened and unwilling horses and mules. Branches clutched at the men, tearing holes in their shirts and leggings. In ten hours, the trappers could seldom make more than two or three miles. It was discouraging.

As they struggled on, pack mules and horses fell over cliffs or were crippled or drowned in the flooded creeks. To add to their troubles, unfriendly Indians began following the party. Any trapper who didn't keep up with the rest was in for trouble. Jed moved tirelessly up and down the line of men and animals. "Close up!" he would shout. "Close up! If you don't keep up, you'll be picked off by the Indians."

Each night, the company clerk would make a more and more gloomy report to Jed. One evening he said, "Two men were wounded today. That makes six men wounded in five days. Two of the men are too weak to walk. We've also lost five more horses and mules. That makes twenty-seven animals lost in five days."

Jed put aside his Bible, got up, and moved restlessly about.

Art Black stuck his head out of his blankets. "Wonder when Jed sleeps," he said to the man lying exhausted beside him. "I see him moving about the camp when I go to sleep. I see him up in the morning when the clerk drags me out of my blankets. All day long, Jed moves up and down the line guarding against Indians and looking for a better trail."

"Go to sleep, Art," his neighbor grumbled. "It's no use tryin' to figure out what keeps Old Jed goin' after we're all wore out. He just ain't human, that's all."

Early in June, the ragged men crossed the Klamath River and moved on to the Pacific coast. It was much easier going now. They traveled north close to the beach and were soon in Oregon. Their enemies had been left far behind.

Here, in Oregon, the Indians seemed to be of a friendly sort. They wanted to trade. They brought beaver pelts and elk meat to the trappers' camp and were well satisfied with what they got in exchange. But Jed had learned his lesson. He kept a watchful eye out for any signs of trouble. To his own men he said, "Be careful how you treat the Indians. Our lives depend on how you act."

But on the very first day, things went wrong. After the Indians had finished trading, one of them had gone over to a trapper's horse and stood there examining it. The trapper whose horse it was noticed the Indian and shouted angrily at him to get away. Jed at once hurried there to smooth things over, but the Indian turned and proudly left the camp.

Jed looked sternly at the trapper. "It is no use to whip you for breaking my rule about treating the Indians right," he said. "Whipping doesn't seem to put sense into you fellows. We can only hope that your next mistake does not cause us trouble."

The next morning, Jed called Art Black and another man, John Turner, to one side.

"I don't want to stay here any longer," Jed said. "There is trouble in the air. We will take an Indian guide in a canoe and try to find a trail to the north."

Jed then gave orders to his clerk to watch the Indians closely in case any of them came to the camp while he was away.

The three men and their guide traveled up a small stream. They had gone some little distance when Jed spotted a place where the river could be crossed. He began to turn the canoe around to start back to camp.

All at once the Indian guide, whom they had not thought of watching, gave the canoe a savage jerk that threw the men into the river. When Jed, Art, and John Turner came to the surface, they realized this was no accident. Indians were firing at them from the bank.

"Dive and swim for the other side!" shouted Jed.

Whoops and shots followed them as they held their breath and swam. By some miracle, they reached the opposite bank safely. Jed, with the others, immediately hurried to a near- by hill and turned his eyes in the direction of the camp.

From there sounds of battle could be clearly heard. He took one look, then pushed the other men back. "It's no use," he said sadly. "They have killed every man. There is nothing we can do but head north as fast as we can go."

For days, the three men lived on roots and berries. Jed and his companions were nearly dead from hunger by the time they reached Fort Vancouver, the trading post of the Hudson's Bay Company on the Columbia River. A French Canadian trapper who met them in the wilderness brought them into the fort.

Dr. John McLoughlin, headman at the fort, looked grave when he heard the story Jed had to tell. His deep voice rumbled, the long white hair that fell over his shoulders shook as he spoke. For the "White-Headed Eagle," as the Indians respectfully called him, was very angry.

"You Americans have caused us trouble, Mr. Smith," he said. "You have been trapping in the Oregon country that we consider to be our land. And you have stirred up the Indians. We have no trouble with Indians. We treat them firmly but fairly, and they trust us. They even come to the fort when they are sick. I give them medicine. Now you have made things difficult for us."

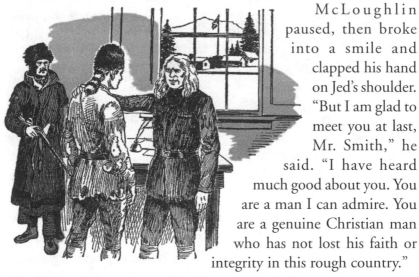

McLoughlin paused, then broke into a smile and clapped his hand on Jed's shoulder. "But I am glad to meet you at last, Mr. Smith," he said. "I have heard much good about you. You are a man I can admire. You are a genuine Christian man who has not lost his faith or integrity in this rough country."

The "White-Headed Eagle" picked up his cane and hurried out on the porch. "McLeod! McLeod!" he roared. "Where in thunder is McLeod?"

A tall, slim man stepped from a nearby cabin.

"McLeod," said McLoughlin, "an American trapper has been robbed. All his men have been killed. Take fifty men and twenty packhorses and go to the Umpqua River. Now, go! Hurry! God bless you." The "White-Headed Eagle" then stamped back to his office to see what he could do to make Jed and his two men comfortable.

Early in December, McLeod's men returned to Fort Vancouver. With the help of Starnoose, an Umpqua Indian chief, they had recovered much of Jed's property.

During the winter, which Jed and his men spent at the fort, Sir George Simpson, governor general of the Hudson's Bay Company, came to visit. He talked for some time with Jed.

"It cost us several thousand dollars," Sir George said, "to recover your property." Then, as Jed looked away uncomfortably, he added quickly, "But we want no repayment. We are glad we were able to help you."

"You are very kind, Sir George," Jed replied. "I hope that in a small way I can be helpful to you in turn. I should like to tell you what I have learned about the trails and fur-trapping lands in California. You also have my promise to stay out of your trapping lands."

"What did I tell you, Sir George," boomed McLoughlin. "This Mr. Smith is a Christian gentleman and a very rare fellow besides! He offers us valuable information that I know we can trust!"

After that, Jed felt better about staying on at the fort, but as soon as spring came he got ready to leave. Art was anxious to leave too, but John Turner said he wanted to stay on at Fort Vancouver.

"In that case," Jed said, "we'll go on without you."

"The trails to the east are dangerous!" the "White-Headed Eagle" warned. "It is madness for two men to attempt such a trip. You had better wait until you can join a Hudson's Bay Company expedition."

But Jed would not wait.

Traveling by night and hiding from Indians during the day, the two trappers followed the Columbia River north as far as Clark's

Fork. Then they journeyed south and east toward the Snake River.

One day when they were already well on their way, Jed suddenly saw, a little distance away, several forms moving towards them along the trail. He quickly drew Art behind a tree. Finger on trigger, they stood silently peering into the forest. All at once Jed cried out joyfully, "Don't shoot, Art. That's Dave Jackson out there." Holding his rifle over his head, Jed stepped out into the trail.

The partners shook hands solemnly while the other trappers were slapping Art on the back.

"You've been gone a right smart time," Dave said quietly to Jed. "We decided to do a little huntin' for you."

"I'm glad you did, Dave," Jed said just as quietly.

Art Black suddenly began to laugh. He laughed and couldn't stop laughing while the others wondered what it was all about. "Those two!" Art got out at last. "They talk like they had met after a short trip down to the store for a pound of sugar! Don't you fellows ever get excited about anything?"

"Jed knows I'm glad to see him," Dave answered. "Ain't no reason for me to throw my hat in the air to show it."

CHAPTER 16

"The Greatest of the Mountain Men"

In December of 1829, Smith and his partners, Dave Jackson and William Sublette, were in camp near the Wind River.

Jed was sitting in his lodge thinking about his future. He was getting tired of a wandering life. He had been to the unknown regions he had dreamed about. He had mapped the great country between the Colorado and the Columbia rivers. Soon settlers would be moving into that country, and it would become part of the United States. It was time to quit, settle down, and do something for his family.

"After the next rendezvous, I'll retire," he said to himself. A farm in Ohio was what would suit him now—a farm and a chance to help his younger brothers get a start in life. Yes, after the rendezvous of 1830 he would retire.

The partners were making big plans for this next rendezvous, which would be held right there on Wind River. William Sublette was to go to St. Louis to buy goods, but this time he was to bring them up in freight wagons. William was all excited by the idea of freight wagons.

"On the Santa Fe Trail, freight wagons have been used for many years," he said. "But this will be the first time that wagons ever have come into this country. I can bring more goods by using freight wagons. Then afterwards we can take our furs back to St. Louis in them. We won't have to risk losing furs in the Missouri River or to the Blackfoot Indians."

"It's a good idea," said Jed. "But I'm worried about that winter trip to St. Louis. Winter travel in this country is dangerous."

"Listen to who's talking about danger!" said Sublette, laughing. "The man who crossed the Sierra Nevada Mountains in seven feet of snow is worrying about a trip to St. Louis! Well, don't worry, Jed, I'm taking 'Black' Harris with me. He's made this trip many times during the winter."

That spring, Jed led a party of trappers north to the Musselshell River, where he had spent his first winter in the mountains. By summer, with a large number of fur packs, he headed south for the Wind River rendezvous. "Black" Harris had returned from St. Louis to say that Sublette was on his way. Sublette had ten 1800-pound wagons loaded with goods prized by trappers and Indians.

Men moved ahead of the wagons, clearing a road through the wilderness. Behind them came other men driving beef cattle and a cow, to supply fresh milk. Indians stared in amazement. They had never seen a wagon. Many had never seen a cow!

From far and near trappers came, leading packhorses loaded with furs. Indians came riding on shaggy ponies. Everyone had pelts to exchange for the wonderful things brought from St. Louis in the freight wagons.

When the rendezvous was over, Jed, Dave, and William had

$25,000 worth of furs to pack into their wagons. They also had a note for $15,132 paid by a group of mountain men to whom the partners had sold their fur trapping business. In their own eyes, and in the eyes of all the trappers, they were rich men.

The mountain men cheered wildly as Jed said good-bye. Some even wiped away a few tears. They were tough, rough trappers, but they loved "Old Jed."

"There ain't a man here who's mad because Jed made money and he didn't," said one mountain man. "We all know that Old Jed took his chances along with the rest of us. He saved his scalp from the Indians because he was a good man. He didn't depend on someone else to do his fightin' for him."

Art Black was going away, too—he couldn't see staying in the wilderness without Jed. "It won't be any fun when you aren't around, Jed," he said. "Maybe, if I try real hard, I can settle down in St. Louis for a spell."

People crowded the streets of St. Louis when Jed and his partners arrived with their freight wagons. Everybody wanted to look at the men who had got rich in the fur trapping business. It was like a parade. And the next day, the St. Louis Beacon had a long story about Jed and Dave and William.

"We understand," the paper said, "that these gentlemen have done well. They brought in a large amount of furs and were richly rewarded for their courage and the dangers they ran. Mr. Smith has been out five years and has explored the country from the Gulf of California to the mouth of the Columbia. We hope soon to be able to give a more particular account of these gentlemen and of the country they have explored."

Jed was not greatly interested in what the newspaper had to say. He was busy doing some of the things that had lately filled his mind. He was arranging for his brothers, Benjamin, Ira, and Nelson, to go to school. He was buying a silver table service to send to Louisa Smith, daughter of Dr. Simons. He was sending money to his father and Dr. Simons and presenting a large gift to a St. Louis church.

For himself, Jed was making plans to be a farmer. Right soon now he would look up Jim Clyman and see how he was making out on his Missouri farm.

In between times, Jed was writing. He had kept careful records of his trips, and now he was writing a book all about the trails he had discovered in the West.

One day while Jed was working on this book, a messenger entered saying that a newspaper reporter wished to talk to Mr. Smith. William Sublette was visiting Jed at the time. Jed said to him, "I don't want to turn anyone away from my door, William. But I must finish this book before I leave for Ohio. Please go out and talk to the reporter. Tell him I will try to see him later."

"I think I can talk about you better than you can, Jed," William replied. "I'll go see him. He'll get a story for his paper all right!"

"I am grateful to you, Mr. Sublette," the reporter said after they had talked for an hour. "I think I have the facts straight now.

Jed Smith was the first American to make his way into California from the East. He was the first American to travel out of California from the West and across the Sierra Nevada Mountains. He was the first man to cross the Great Salt Lake Desert."

The reporter thought a moment, then said, "All those things are very fine, Mr. Sublette. Newspaper readers will read them and believe them. But will they believe these other things you told me?

"Jed Smith, the leader of rough mountain men, never took a drink or used bad language. He broke holes in the ice to get water to shave in. He read his Bible nearly every night and liked to sing Methodist hymns as he rode through the wilderness. He was gentle, but he could lick any trapper who disobeyed him."

The reporter looked hard at William Sublette and shook his head doubtfully. "Newspaper readers simply won't believe those things if I write them, Mr. Sublette!" he said.

William Sublette smiled. "I know, son, it's hard for you to believe what I tell you about Jed. You weren't there. Even for us who were there and saw him, it was hard to believe that a man could be so tough and yet so gentle. I heard one mountain man put it this way: 'Old Jed is half preacher and half grizzly bear!'"

William Sublette thought a moment. Then he said, "I'll tell you what, son. Write it like this. It is the truth, the whole truth. Jed Smith was a true trailblazer—the greatest of the mountain men. There will never be another like him in all the West."